Pictorial Guide to Chautauqua

A family destination and a
center for the arts, education,
religion and recreation

Fountain before
Post Office by Fred Torrey

"There is no place like it. No resort. No spa. Not anywhere else in the country, or anywhere in the world; it is at once a summer encampment and a small town, a college campus, an arts colony, a music festival, a religious retreat and a village square – and there's no place – no place – with anything like its history."
by Historian David Gaub McCullough

"It began with two men who shared common values, complementary resources, and a vision to create 'a place, an idea, and a force.' In 1874, their vision became reality: a summer community dedicated to education, religion, science and the arts."
by Archivist Marilyn M. Bendiksen

"This place embodies the life we wish we could always live."
by Justice Sandra Day O'Connor

"Chautauqua has it all! – a kind of Gestalt experience."
by Conductor Nathan Gottschalk

"The thing that brings so much joy to my heart is when people discover Chautauqua. It really makes no difference if they are a Noble Peace Prize winner, or an accordionist or ventriloquist, or an ambassador. It's that all people who stay here walk away with a love of Chautauqua."
by Hostess Rachel Mazza Borzilleri

What is Chautauqua? "The most American thing in America"
by President Theodore Roosevelt

"The Chautauqua Experience at its core is educational. The vigorous symphony of life awakens Chautauquans - in an audience of thousands at the Amphitheater or during a quiet read on a shaded porch. The mind stretches, the senses come alive, and the spirit is enriched."
by Chautauqua VP Richard Redington

TABLE OF CONTENTS

FIRST IMPRESSIONS

by Richard N. Campen, Architectural Historian

"In the course of touring Austria, perhaps at Bad Ischl, the beautiful strains of a Viennese waltz reached my ears. In a well fenestrated pavilion a string orchestra was playing the lilting music of Strauss, Lanner, Lehar and others so reminiscent of the gay, carefree Vienna of Franz Josef. It was peopled by couples . . . seated, relaxed, listening. It was beautiful! – the music, the scene. I have never experienced such a dignified, civilized passing of time before. Chautauqua reminds me of that memorable, serendipitous, Austrian encounter. . . Chautauqua, too, is a most civilized place."

DESIGN BY SELDEN CAMPEN

Copyright © 2016 by Selden W. Campen
All rights reserved
Library of Congress Number: 2016904881
ISBN: 978-0-9973936-0-6
Self Published in Chautauqua, New York
Printed in the United States of America
by Falconer Printing and Design Inc.
Typeface: Minion Pro
Paper: Endurance 80# Silk Text
Cover stock: Endurance 120# Silk Cover
        with Flood Coat Satin Varnish

For all information contact:
Selden W. Campen
Telephone: (412) 865-7341
Email: swcampen@msn.com

Acknowledgements

Work on *Pictorial Guide to Chautauqua* began in 2010, and I am completing it 6 years later, in time for the 2016 season. When I had commented to Michael Sullivan, then Chautauqua Director of Institution Relations, that the existing *Official Walking Tour Guidebook of the Chautauqua Institution* was out of date and lacked color, he encouraged me to write a new walking tour guide. Many thanks to Mr. Sullivan for starting me on this project and providing access to Chautauqua-owned text and media, and to George Murphy, current Chautauqua Chief Marketing Officer, for continuing this same open access.

In assembling *Pictorial Guide to Chautauqua*, I liberally reworked and/or transcribed text from: Richard Campen's *Chautauqua Impressions*, Chautauqua Institution's The Chautauquan Daily, previous walking tours, marketing brochures, Visitors Center exhibits, Pauline Francher's *Chautauqua: Its Architecture and Its People*, Google sites (too many to track), and Alfreda Irwin's *Three Taps of the Gavel*.

I tried my hand at original research via use of the Chautauqua Grapevine in the form of a Q&A during the Spring of 2013. Thus many facts from the first hand knowledge of numerous Chautauquans are incorporated into this guide.

Inserting photos into the text became easy due the generosity of many Chautauquans, namely: The Baptist House (James Huron), Gena Bedrosian, Donna Brenner, Robert Cahn, Roger Coda, Robert Davis, Ray Downey, Eve Edelheit, The Everett Jewish Life Center (Richard Spivak), Demetrius Freeman, Greg Funka, Michael Gelfield, Christopher Gibbs, Bria Granville, Ellie Haugsby, Diane Hess, Benjamin Host, Caroline Jahrling, Darlyne Johnston, Norman Karp, Saalik Khan, Matt Kleck, Carolyn Lingenfeler, Ernie Mahaffey, Roxana Pop, Caitlin Prarat, Rosemary Rappole, Carol Rizzolo, Josette Rolley, Farley Toothman Ruby Wallau, Jeanne Wiebenga and Kreable Young.

Paintings and graphic art were enthusiastically provided by Deborah Blodgett, Mary Ann Boyson, Jerome Chesley, The Fabulous Shirtheads (Mikel, Dan and Peter Wintermantel), Robert Jeffrey and Robin Robins.

To all of these individuals and organizations, I am indebted; the efforts of many are more interesting than that of one. I used Adobe InDesign to assemble material from all of these sources.

Arnold Halpern's assistance in balancing the color, brightness and intensity of the graphics in first third of the book during the 2015 season illustrated the importance of this function which eventually was fulfilled by Lisa Short at Falconer Printing and Design. Their contributions significantly improved the book's visual appeal.

Many Chautauquans reviewed the text related to their own property. In addition Bill Flanders and Marlie Bendiksen, who have worked for many years with Chautauqua Institution's Oliver Archives Center, performed a broader review for which I am grateful.

As I am a banker by trade, writing did not come easy. A special thanks to my wife, Jacqueline, who was the first to review the text, providing suggestions for enhancement, and to Alice O'Grady, who polished it to be the literate text expected of a work about Chautauqua. A special thanks to each of these individuals.

Finally I'd like to thank Alice O'Grady again, this time for writing the Foreward to *Pictorial Guide to Chauutauqua*. Alice, a local resident, had worked more than 14 years as a reporter for The Chautauquan Daily and is knowledgeable about Chautauqua's history and other writings on its past.

In compiling this book I learned much about Chautauqua; in reading it I hope you will as well.

Selden Campen, Author and Publisher
March 2016

Dedication

This book is dedicated to my seven grandchildren: Amber, Cicely, Cooper, Elijah, Jackson, Nathan and Olivia. May they in due course come to appreciate the performing and visual arts, the written and oral word, and the recreational opportunities that together comprise the "mix" that is Chautauqua.

Jason Weintraub,
Community Band
Conductor

Photo by Jeanne Wiebenga

Foreward

Having spent the past twenty summers at Chautauqua Institution—fourteen of them as a reporter for The Chautauquan Daily—and sixteen winters nearby, you might expect me to have become familiar with most of the buildings here. I do know the Institution structures well, but private dwellings less so.

Therefore I look forward to strolling around the grounds with Selden Campen's book in hand. I anticipate becoming familiar not only with the exterior features of many of the residences, but learning also of their construction and their history. Which ones are hiding an old tent platform beneath them? What architectural style is this one, and what famous Chautauquan lived—or lives—in that one?

This book is a walking tour of the grounds, and even calls attention to a few places nearby. Campen is thorough in his coverage of public spaces and representative in discussing private spaces, including cottages, manor houses, rooming houses, denominational houses and dormitories. The mentions of who built them and who resided there read like a Who's Who in America. There are stories of how the persons referenced participated in and supported the Institution, thus highlighting the reality of our community.

Another feature of this book is that it captures much of the everyday lives of the people who visit and those who live here. Folks eating ice cream cones, selling newspapers, playing a musical instrument, shopping at the flea market, touring Palestine Park, attending a lecture, pumping the Tallman organ, or getting married are among those pictured. They all happen here, and they, as well as many other activities, are documented forever in this book's lovely photographs.

Many have written excellent books about Chautauqua. Jesse Hurlbut, Alfreda Irwin and Jeffrey Simpson have thoroughly documented Chautauqua Institution's history, while Pauline Francher and Richard Campen identified its architecture. Laurie Watters provided a photographic portrayal of Chautauqua. Each author's work illustrated a specific aspect of this place.

However, in this book you will find a balanced composite of Chautauqua's history, architecture and culture. It has something for everyone: residents and guests, adults and youth, sailors, opera buffs, lecture attendees and students of all ages among them. And if you want to read about a certain address or homeowner, the index, not always included in such books, can be quite useful.

The six-year effort that went into organizing such a font of information is impressive. Campen spent much of that time taking many of the lovely photos in the book and gathering interesting images from others. You will find not only photos of locations, but of some paintings as well. He has gathered gems of information from numerous publications and experts; refer to the bibliography to appreciate the extent of his research.

A lot of this "research" could also be called first-hand experience. Having initially come to Chautauqua thirty-four years ago, his experience here has provided him with a feeling for the culture and ambiance of the place, as well as many specific details. Much of this is reflected in these pages.

So if you should see me wandering and gazing, book in hand, please don't run me over with your bicycle. Know that I'm busy absorbing Chautauqua.

Alice R. O'Grady
March 2016

The Chautauqua Experience

For nine weeks each year, from late June through late August, the Chautauqua Institution offers an extraordinary blend of programming in the arts, education, religion and recreation. It is at once a community, a renowned center for the performing arts and a resource for the discussion of the important issues of our time. The Institution encompasses 750 acres on the shore of Chautauqua Lake in southwestern New York State. A National Historic District, it attracts 100,000 visitors during a season of more than 2,200 events.

Historian and author David McCullough said about Chautauqua, "There is no place like it. No resort. No spa. Not anywhere else in the country, or anywhere in the world; it is at once a summer encampment and a small town, a college campus, an arts colony, a music festival, a religious retreat and a village square – and there's no place – no place – with anything like its history."

Originally called the Chautauqua Lake Sunday School Assembly, the Institution was founded in 1874 as an educational experiment in out-of-school, vacation learning. It was conceived in 1874 by John Heyl Vincent, a devout Methodist minister, who later became a bishop and editor of the nationally circulated *Sunday School Journal* and Lewis Miller, a successful manufacturer of farm equipment for the developing Midwest. The "Chautauqua Idea" was and is profound; to make widely available learning that involves the mind, spirit and body, that is unrestricted by age, topic or discipline, and that is inspired by a community devoted entirely to the free pursuit of learning.

Miller and Vincent leased 50 acres of land from the Chautauqua Lake Camp Meeting Association at Fair Point on Chautauqua Lake and organized an intensive two-week study course for Sunday school teachers. Their idea of combining religious study with academic subjects, music, art, and physical education was unique and immediately successful. The peaceful setting on the lake, the abundance of railroads in the area, and a fleet of steamboats that serviced the lake made Fair Point a desirable location.

The Chautauqua Idea rapidly caught the interest of the nation. Ultimately, in what became known as the Chautauqua Movement, the Idea spread to millions of people of modest means who sought information and strove for enlightenment not otherwise available to them. Within a generation, 150 permanent Chautauquas had sprung up, and traveling tent Chautauquas traversed the country. Hundreds of thousands of Americans enrolled in what has become one of the country's oldest continuously operating book clubs, the Chautauqua Literary and Scientific Circle.

As a program center, Chautauqua attracts participants who expect to be actively involved and intellectually challenged by a variety of programs. As a community, Chautauqua displays the virtues of civil dialogue, the pursuit of excellence and the understanding of others based upon personal relationships.

Several cultural critics have made the observation that Chautauqua during the nine-week season is appropriately compared, not to an arts festival or seminar site, but to major cities such as New York or Chicago. It is rightly understood as a cultural metropolis presenting the full range of artistic, educational, spiritual, and recreational expressions of contemporary civilization. Chautauquans simply call it "the mix," and know it is the whole, not any one of these parts, that makes "The Chautauqua Experience" what it is.

A host of leading thinkers and political leaders, national and global, have said that Chautauqua inspires them in a way nothing else can. As Justice Sandra Day O'Connor has written, it embodies the "life we wish we could always live."

Chautauqua's signature program, the lecture series, has hosted distinguished Americans from all walks of life. Susan B. Anthony argued here for women's suffrage in 1892, Franklin Roosevelt gave his "I Hate War" speech here in 1936. More recently astronaut Jim Irwin, Ambassador Dennis Ross, educator Michael Sandel, Justice Thurgood Marshall, author Alex Haley, geographer Harm de Blij, historian Jay Winik, and coach Tara VanDerveer have all spoken here.

This *Pictorial Guide to Chautauqua* displays images of the buildings and spaces of the Institution. It is intended to be used as a walking tour of the grounds and for this purpose includes a map on the inside back cover. Subsequently, when leaving the grounds, it is hoped you will use this book to share the beauty and ambiance of Chautauqua Institution with others who have not yet had the opportunity to experience Chautauqua first hand.

Chautauqua Founders Lewis Miller (left) and John Heyl Vincent (right)

Photo from www.wikipedia.com   Photo from SMU Bridwell Lib. Archives

Main Gate Welcome Center – 1917

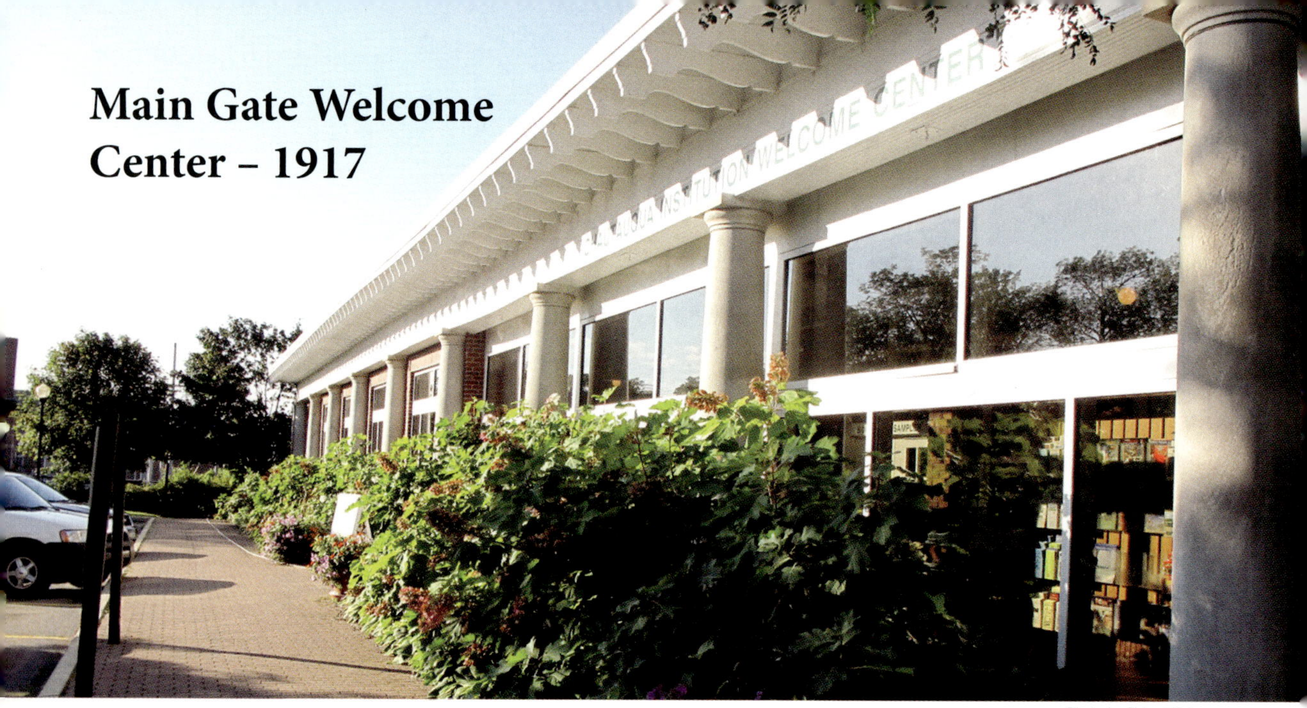

Photo by Robert Cahn

The Main Gate Welcome Center was originally built as a trolley car station in 1917. The trolley line ran from Jamestown at the south end of the lake, through Mayville, to Westfield, where it connected with the interurban line running along the south shore of Lake Erie. At its founding and for the next quarter century, the main access to Chautauqua was via water to Fair Point. Gradually trolley and then auto became the primary mode of transportation to Chautauqua, so the Road Gate, as it was once known, became the Main Gate. It was reconfigured and expanded in 1997 and now, as an enclosed year-round facility, it houses the Chautauqua County Visitor's Bureau, the Chautauqua Institution's ticketing offices and the Chautauqua Bookstore Sampler.

Photo by Selden Campen

Photo by Robert Cahn

Photo by Robert Cahn

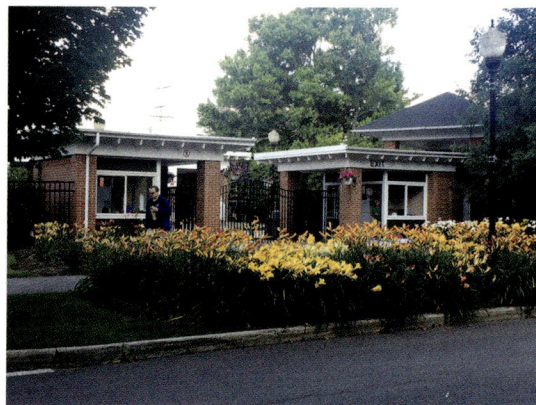

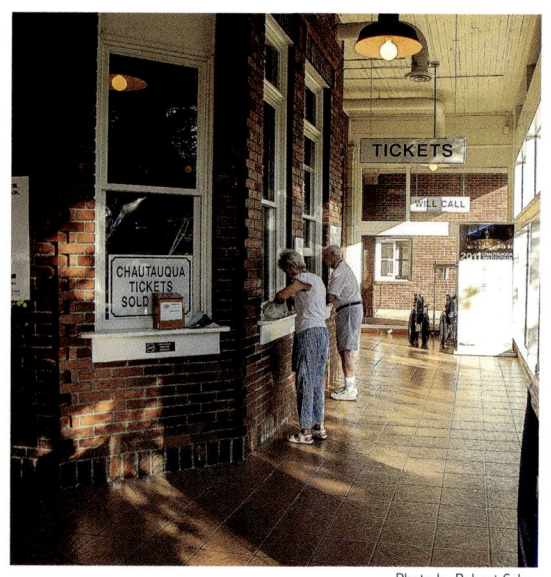

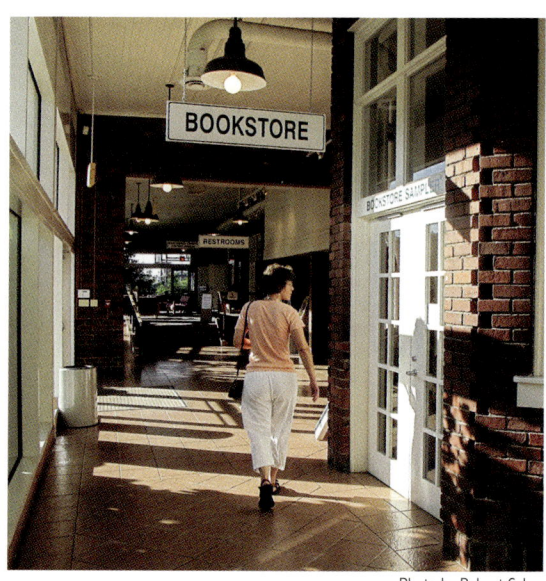

People call Chautauqua a Victorian village, but it is actually quite eclectic, having more than twenty architectural styles. Chautauqua is Victorian in the sense that it is a pedestrian community with narrow streets not designed for cars or buses. Houses are close together and nearly every house has a front porch that enables easy communication with neighbors. Many of the homes have plaques stating the year of construction.

Vincent Avenue

This photo looking west toward the Main Gate on **Vincent Avenue** illustrates the near universal use of front porches and the mature tree cover which together are significant factors creating the ambiance at Chautauqua. This and several other major avenues are paved in brick, which denotes reserved for pedestrian traffic. In the opposite direction on the other side of Bestor Plaza, Vincent Avenue extends down the hill to Miller Park and Chautauqua Lake.

Photo by Selden Campen

Bestor Plaza

This lovely village square is named **Bestor Plaza** to honor Dr. Arthur E. Bestor, the Institution's longest serving president, from 1915 to 1944. He led Chautauqua through two world wars and the Great Depression, when it actually went into receivership in 1933. Prior to Bestor's time, Chautauqua was focused on the training of Sunday school teachers. Under his leadership, the arts were emphasized and Chautauqua became a model for music festivals that would become popular in the decades to follow. Bestor was a genuinely friendly man who allowed himself time for conversation as he frequently made his way from his office to the Amphitheater. It was a natural tribute to name this central park in his honor.

Photo from "Chautauqua Salute" by Mary Frances Bestor Cram

Now Bestor Plaza is a meeting place for young and old alike. At the center is a fountain with a four-sided shaft designed in 1946 by Chicagoan Fred Torrey, who also executed the relief sculpture on the facade of Norton Hall and the fountain before the Post Office Building. The fountain design illustrates Chautauqua's emphasis on Religion, Knowledge, Music, and Art. The Plaza is surrounded by the major edifices of the Institution and is graced at either end by colorful gardens. The mature shade trees make it a comfortable place to observe life as people hurry by to fetch mail, attend lectures, or come to throw frisbees, make conversation with friends, or enjoy an ice cream cone. As part of the 125th anniversary celebration, historical markers have been erected in the plaza describing other buildings that once occupied the space.

Bestor Plaza fountain sculpted by Fred Torrey: Religion (south) and Art (west) surfaces are pictured.

Photo by Richard Campen

Life on the Plaza

July 4th Community Band concert conducted by Jason Weintraub

Photo by Robert Cahn

Photo by Jeanne Wiebenga

Picnic lunch following morning lecture

Photo by Richard Campen

Newspaper boy sells The Chautauquan Daily

Photo by Selden Campen

Developing new skills

Photo by Michael Gelfield

Dancing in period attire – Victorian Tennis Day

Photo by Selden Campen

The Chautauqua Alliance Craft Show

Photo by Selden Campen

Children's School story hour

Photo by Selden Campen

The Colonnade

Photo by Jeanne Wiebenga

Colonnade – 1905

Facing the Plaza, the large concrete pillars and Georgian classical revival style of the **Colonnade** at **1 Ames** give it a gracious, imposing appearance. The walkway between its Ionic columns and the building's facade gives the Colonnade its name. Chautauqua Institution's administration offices are located on the second floor and many shops are on the first floor along with the offices of the Chautauqua Foundation, the Institution's ticketing offices, and a concierge counter to assist visitors with information about the campus and activities on the grounds.

Photo by Richard Campen

To build this 90-foot by 173-foot structure, it was necessary to move the Anne M. Kellogg Memorial Hall, now known as the Fowler-Kellogg Art Center. The Colonnade was first built at a cost of $35,000 in 1905, rebuilt after a fire in 1907, and restored again following another fire in 1961. Institution President William J. Carothers oversaw its reconstruction in time for the 1961 season, just 5 months after the second devastating fire.

The Colonnade was designed by Buffalo architect E. B. Green. His firm, Green and Wicks, was responsible for construction of eleven buildings on the grounds between 1905 and 1916.

On the brick facade to the right of the pillars is the Annual Chautauqua Fund thermometer measuring the progress of the current year's fund drive.

Photo by Selden Campen

Post Office / Bookstore / Afterwords Café - 1909

In 1877 a post office was established at Fair Point and soon after, perhaps the same year, the community was granted permission to change its name to Chautauqua. Taking the name Chautauqua was a logical step, as the Assembly was already making the name of the lake famous.

The current **Post Office building** was designed and built by E. B. Green in 1909. As with many of the major structures at Chautauqua, design and construction occurred within the nine-month period between Chautauqua seasons. The U.S. Post Office has been a continual tenant since the building's inception. The print shop for the newspaper and CLSC materials was originally located in the English basement below the Post Office.

In 1974 the U.S. Postal Service honored Chautauqua during its centennial celebration with the issuance of a 10¢ stamp picturing the traveling Chautauqua tents that brought Institution speakers such as William Jennings Bryan to rural America.

Chautauquans appreciate their post office and especially the last several postmistresses, who go out of their way to offer extraordinary service. Chautauquans honored their post office by launching a successful campaign in 2000 to have it uniquely declared The All American Post Office.

The **Chautauqua Bookstore** has had a migratory career, having been located in the Arcade, what is now the Hultquist Center, and the Colonnade before moving to the Post Office building. For the past 80 years or more, it has occupied the building's lower level. In addition to its excellent collection of books, it offers unique gift items and souvenirs. Vendor of The Chautauquan Daily and dailies of Jamestown, Buffalo, Cleveland, Pittsburgh and New York City, it is one of the most important "ports-of-call" for visitors and Chautauquans alike.

To the left of and on the same level as the Post Office is an Institution operated coffee bar and sandwich shop known as the **Afterwords Café**. In the right wing of the upper level is the **Chautauqua Visitors Center**.

Photo by Jeanne Wiebenga

Photo by Selden Campen

Photo by Richard Campen

Brick Walk Café (formerly The Refectory) – 1945

Coincident with the Refectory's construction in 1945, Bestor Plaza was extended to include its current southwest corner. Refectory, meaning dining hall in a college or institution, proved to be a rather exalted name for the place where Chautauquans bought their ice cream cones, but the red brick building is an attractive addition to the Plaza. The **Refectory** replaced the Pergola, an open-air ice cream parlor and merchant stand, which previously stood on the northeast corner of the Plaza adjacent to the Colonnade. In 1973, the Welch Foods Company assumed management of the Refectory and rebranded it **Welch's Refreshment Pavilion**.

Starting soon thereafter in 1974, under the aw-ning on the right front of the building, Jim Roselle and Jamestown radio station WJTN have maintained an open air studio in which nearly all of Chautauqua's morning lecturers have been interviewed before their 10:45 AM appearance in the Amphitheater. In 2012, after another major interior and exterior renovation focused upon improving the ambiance while increasing capacity and food selection, the building reopened as the **Brick Walk Café**. Roselle's interviews are now conducted in the Author's Alcove between the Post Office and the Brick Walk Cafe.

On Miller Avenue to the right of the building is a gazebo decorated with Chautauqua scenes painted by local artist Deborah Blodgett.

The Refectory as viewed in 2011 from the Smith Memorial Library balcony.

Photo by Selden Campen

Welch's Pavilion ice cream counter as configured in the 1970's thru mid-80's.

Photo by Robert Cahn

Brick Walk Café Gazebo Art Panel of the Fair Point Pier Building

Painting by Deborah Blodgett

Smith Memorial Library – 1931

So important to this community of readers, **Smith Memorial Library** at **21 Miller Avenue** occupies the entire south side of Bestor Plaza opposite the Colonnade Building. The library, part of the Cattaraugus Library System, is open to the public year-round. For many the library is a daily stop to catch up on the news of the day and/or to meet friends while en route to the morning lecture.

Addie Mae Smith Wilkes

Photo from Chautauqua Archives

In the Georgian Revival style, it was built in 1931 with funds supplied by Mrs. Addie Mae Smith Wilkes. The building's architect was Franklyn Kidd, a student of E. B. Green, architect of the Colonnade. The brickwork and the use of horizontal beams at the entrance endow the building with its character. The Smith Memorial Library's collection consists of over 50,000 volumes.

The first floor consists of one room illuminated by great windows on all sides. It is a pleasant space to browse or engage in serious research. During the summer its central space has a table of Institution-related brochures, while off-season a baby grand piano is available for any patron to use. In keeping with the Institution being a resource for all ages, the first floor of the library holds its fiction and children's collections.

A dual staircase on its central axis leads first to a landing with a Palladian window and then on to the second floor. This floor houses the Library's non-fiction collection, audio CDs of nearly all lectures presented at the Institution during the last decade, computers for public use and some Institution-owned historical artifacts.

As with the post office, Chautauquans love their library. The Friends of the Library annually host a festive Library Day. Juice and donuts are served on the front elevated steps; entertainment is provided by Chautauqua's own *Summer Strummers*.

Photo by Robert Cahn

Photo by Jeanne Wiebenga

Photo by Jeanne Wiebenga

The Grange – 1903

Descending down Miller hill at the corner with Simpson is **the Grange.** Originally this structure at **8 Simpson** served as a social and educational center for farmers – note that "Patrons of Husbandry" is inscribed across the frieze. It is of the Greek Revival Style, evidenced by the shallow roof, the broad frieze board under the eaves and the Doric columns. Stylistically it is an anachronism. It might well have been built in the 1850s, rather than 1903, when in America the Greek Revival Style had largely spent itself.

The Grange, original owners of this cottage, was founded in nearby Fredonia in 1868. "Grange Day" was celebrated at Chautauqua on August third for many years until the building was converted into a private dwelling.

Entry to the Grange is via the old meeting room, 20 feet by 30 feet with 18 foot ceilings. In the kitchen, entered through a doorway at the left rear, is an interesting stained glass window added by the Whaley family. It depicts the Grange cottage, the Athenaeum Hotel, the Miller Bell Tower, musicians working their trade, and a sailboat. A whale (for Whaley) can be made out above the sailboat.

Photo by Selden Campen

Rutherford B. Hayes addressed the Grange at Chautauqua on August 19, 1892 in the Ampitheater after staying the night before in the Athenaeum Hotel.

Photo by Selden Campen

Photo by Selden Campen

Photo by Jeanne Wiebenga

Photo by Michael Gelfield

Hultquist Center – 1889/1999

The Assembly Herald Building at **19 Miller Avenue**, now known as the **Hultquist Center,** was erected in 1889. It initially housed the Chautauqua Assembly Herald daily newspaper (becoming The Chautauquan Daily in 1907) and the monthly magazine The Chautauquan. Later it briefly served as the Institution's administration center, until those functions were moved to the Colonnade. From 1911 through 1998 the building was used for retail sales and was known as the Oriental Bazaar. It was then converted with funds from the Hultquist family for year-round classroom/conference center use and gained its current name.

At the south end of the building is the CLSC Veranda, the headquarters and bookstore for the Chautauqua Literary and Scientific Circle. At the Veranda one can join one of the oldest book clubs in the United States, get a listing of its selections since its founding in 1878, or simply purchase one of the current year's books. Anyone having read 16 of the CLSC books and paid dues for four years is eligible to graduate and participate in graduation day festivities.

Brick Walk leading to Hultquist Center with Refectory (left) and Florida Fountain (right)

Photo by Selden Campen

Photo by Robert Cahn

Meet and greet Special Studies instructors on brick walk by Hultquist Center each Sunday afternoon.

Photo by Selden Campen

CLSC Veranda at 19 Clark Avenue

Photo by Robert Cahn

The Amphitheater -1893

"Is there room for one more?" This question is frequently asked on big program nights at the Chautauqua Amphitheater when seven thousand try to crowd into the bowl while another thousand wait around the rim hoping to see an opening somewhere. The Amphitheater comfortably seats 5,600. Bleachers at the rear, removed in 2016, accommodated another 500.

The **Amphitheater** is almost continually in use during daylight hours, if not for scheduled programs, then for rehearsals. Few podiums in the country have hosted more noted performers and speakers. The popular "Sunday at Chautauqua" religious services are held in the Amphitheater weekly in season and are open for the public to attend at no charge.

Board Chairman Howard Gibbs made these remarks upon the repainting of the Amphitheater in July 1982: "In essence the Amphitheater is a place of repose, reflection and renewal – a place to learn, to question, to share; a place where history is made." In 1893, at a then unbelievable cost of $26,000, it replaced an earlier amphitheater built in the same ravine. The Amphitheater is truly at the heart of the Chautauqua program, serving daily as church, lecture platform, and concert hall. It has the distinction of being the oldest and largest open-air, covered amphitheater still in use.

The amphitheater's predecessor, called the Pavilion, came into being in 1887 when the Tabernacle tent was moved to this ravine. The natural half bowl of land was cleared and fitted with benches that faced a platform. Then in 1879 came the first Amphitheater, all wooden,

with posts that blocked the view of many and a roof that was too noisy when it rained. Its cost was $4,500.

In the summer of 1892, little more than a dozen years after construction of the first amphitheater, the Chautauqua Institution trustees approved an entirely new structure. President Lewis Miller had a major role in its planning, financing and execution. It was to be 180 feet long by 160 feet wide with a pitched roof supported by bridge-type trusses bearing on 24 steel posts, 20 of which obstruct stage views from many seats along the side, rear and choir sections. The spacing of the posts is such that there is a central space of 160 feet by 100 feet without columnar support. The laterals extending under the surface of the vast roof are supported at its eaves by bracketed, wooden posts. The structure was fitted out with solid-backed wooden benches, providing excellent visibility as, in tiers, they descend toward the stage. The leak-free roof is said to be sheathed with iron shingles. Whatever the roof may be, sound is deadened so that the program can be heard even in a moderately heavy rainstorm. Sound-deadening air is sealed within the space occupied by the roof-bearing trusses above the tongue-and-grooved wooden ceiling arched over the great-unsupported central space. Acoustically, wood is among the best materials, as borne out by the Amphitheater's excellent auditory characteristics.

An interesting phenomenon at Chautauqua's morning lectures and evening symphonies is the multitude of folks converging on the Amphitheater carrying cushions. Considering the hard wooden seats, these almost

July 4th Children's School parade reaches the Amp stage just before the morning lecture.

The Amphitheater – 1893

Photo by Richard Campen

Steel beams support the ceiling over the Amphitheater's large central bowl.

Photo by Selden Campen

become a necessity for favoring the derriere and have created a market for Chautauqua-inscribed, handled cushions, preferably with pockets to hold the daily program.

The Massey Organ is a memorial to Hart A. Massey by his family. Its installation on July 12, 1907 necessitated the enlargement and rearrangement of the "working end" of the Amphitheater. The son of the donor, Chester D. Massey, was a brother-in-law of Chautauqua founder Bishop Vincent.

The organ, considered to be one of the largest "outdoor" organs in the world, consists of 5,628 pipes, the largest being 32 feet long and the smallest about the size of a pencil. It was designed with four manuals of 61 notes each and with a pedal of 32 notes. The organ was rededicated in 1993, after having been completely rehabilitated by the father-and-son team, Paul and Mark Fischer, of the Fischer Organ Company in Erie, Pa.

Additional modifications were made to the original choir loft in 1921 and the stage was widened in 1954. In the backstage area, new rooms were provided for visiting performers as well as storage for instruments, bathrooms were added, and a new roof cover-

Screen House at north west corner of the Amphitheater.

Photo by Selden Campen

ing was installed. In 1964 a new cement floor was cast in place; in 1978 the roof trusses were reinforced and in 1981 bleachers seating 500 persons were added

Walking down Clark Avenue approaching the Amphitheater, one first comes to a gazebo, commonly called the Screen House, managed by the Bookstore. It is here that tapes of the morning speakers may be purchased as well as souvenirs of many of the evening performers.

Currently, consideration is being given by architects as to the best way to enhance the Amphitheater. Three concerns are at the heart of the matter. First, facilitating multimedia presentation that is gradually becoming a requirement of many speakers. Second, enabling a complete view of the platform from all seats by installing truss supports that would eliminate 20 columns. And third, changes to the stage infrastructure that would facilitate easier changeovers from church to lecture platform to evening performances by groups requiring much additional lighting and sound equipment.

Original stage in the 1893 Second Amphitheater

Chautauqua file photo

From this platform on August 11, 1904, William H. Taft addressed Chautauquans about the Phillipines and on August 23, 1905 William McKinley received over 1,500 people on the platform prior to the next days celebration of Grand Army Day.

Several of 5,628 pipes of the Massey Organ

Photo from The Chautauquan Daily – Demetrius Freeman staff photographer

FDR delivering his *I Hate War Speech* in 1936

Chautauqua Archive photo

Proposed Third Ampitheater – Circa 2017

Chautauqua file photo

United Church of Christ – 1931

Built in 1931, the **United Church of Christ** at **6 Bowman Avenue** is uniquely positioned, along with the Presbyterian House, with a view inside the Amphitheater. The leadership of the UCC at Chautauqua describe the house as "Centrally located friendly, family atmosphere, with community kitchen/dining room for self meal preparation, extensive porches, shared bath facilities, sink in each room, buildings upgraded." The UCC also owns the Mayflower House and Reformed Church House. As with most denominational houses on the grounds they offer rooms for rent.

Photo by Selden Campen

Roberts Avenue

Roberts Avenue is a street that has changed very little through the years. It still has a number of rooming houses, which were the norm until the 1980s when many such structures were converted to condominiums.

The Keystone – 1881

Newton Wright built the **Keystone** at **24-26 Roberts** in 1881. Opening one day before the Athenaeum Hotel, it is the oldest rooming house in Chautauqua. Having transported the lumber from Pennsylvania, the Keystone state, with a horse-drawn wagon, he named it the Keystone. The facility grew to include a second building next door at 6 Roberts and a third across the street that is now the Englewood.

When in the late 1960s the Keystone was to have been demolished, Mary Frances Bestor Cram and her husband Ambrose Cram bought it at a state auction. They converted the Keystone from hotel rooms to 18 apartments. In 1980, the building was sold to Bill and Christine Bemus. Bill's grandfather, four generations back, founded nearby Bemus Point in 1803 and operated the ferry at the narrows where the Casino now stands.

Diane Hess organized another substantial renovation, modernization, and upgrade of the Keystone, completed in 1996, that created six year-round apart-

ments, many of which can be subdivided for summer rental purposes. She still resides in the 3rd floor southern-most apartment that, due to its visual and aural connection to the Amphitheater stage, is one of the most desirable residences in all of Chautauqua.

The Keystone in the mid-1980s

Photo by Selden Campen

The Keystone in the early 1900s

Chautauqua archives photo

The Keystone following its reconstruction in 1996

Photo by Diane Hess

Roberts Avenue (Continued)

The Hawthorne – 1875

The residence at **17 Roberts**, one of the most attractive cottages by any measure, occupies the conspicuous location at the intersection with Miller Avenue. Named **The Hawthorne** when it was built, it was known briefly as The Little White House, before the Bechtolts restored the original name. The delicate "wood-lace" bracketing, both upstairs and down, form a series of arches between

the slim attenuated porch columns that assist in imparting a quality of daintiness to the building.

Dick and Nancy Bechtolt purchased 17 Roberts in 1979, where Nancy still resides. In 2006 Dick was awarded the Chautauqua President's Medal for 24 years of consecutive service to the Institution being a member of the Chautauqua Foundation's Board of Directors from 1982-1994 and the Institution's Board of Trustees from 1984 -2006.

The current Unitarian Universalist Fellowship of Chautauqua was formed in 1979 with 25 founding members, among them were Dick and Nancy Bechtolt. Nancy initiated the UU Ethics Lecture Series in 1986, which continues to this day.

Dick Bechtolt had been an avid tennis player and a member of the Dawn Patrol, a group of tennis players who play on the tennis courts from 7 a.m. to 9 a.m. every weekday. Together the UU Fellowship and the Chautauqua Tennis Association recognized Dick's contributions by funding the shelter at the new tennis courts near the Turner Community Center and naming it in his honor.

The Cambridge – 1882

The Cambridge at **9 Roberts** was built in 1882 as a rooming house. In the first half of the 1900s two additional structures on South Terrace were added to the Cambridge operation.

During the 50's, it was 'famous' as Olga's Tea Room. The present owners, Dick and Susan Luehrs, purchased the Cambridge in 1976. They talked with Olga Olsen when she was in her 90s and learned she would routinely get up at four o'clock in the morning to bake 35 pies!

Olson sold the property to Carol (Sundean) and Dick Lewis who purchased it for her parents to manage. It was the Sundeans who named the Cambridge after their hometown, Cambridge Springs, Pa. No longer a tearoom, the Cambridge then offered 28 rooms for rent.

As with many rental properties in the Institution, rooms have and continue to be converted to apartments following the accommodation preferences of Chautauquans. The Cambridge is now configured into nine apartments and seven rooms. In the 1990s the Colden Country Store occupied one of the first floor apartments.

To promote occupancy, Dick and Susan Luehrs have added a spacious covered patio between the buildings, offering complimentary breakfast snacks to guests renting rooms and until recently complimentary bicycle use and sailboat rides for all their guests. All of this contributes to the ambiance that is Chautauqua.

14 South Lake Dr. – 2004

The William Baker Hotel, which stood at the corner of South Lake Drive and Miller Avenue, was renovated along with adjoining structures in 2004 to become residential condos at **14 South Lake**. In 1943 Kenneth W. Baker purchased the Lebanon Hotel and named it for his father. The Lebanon Hotel was built in 1907 and joined to the Fox Cottage, which dates back to the 1880s. Subsequently, Kenneth Baker bought the Belvedere Hotel, also along the lakefront, and used it to further enlarge the William Baker. On the first floor of the William Baker was a popular spacious dining room long enjoyed by Chautauquans.

Six story condo and adjoining new cottages on the William Baker Hotel site

Photo by Selden Campen

The Arcade – 1891

This sizable structure at **4 South Lake Drive** was erected at a cost of only $10,000 in 1891. In 1986 it was converted into 16 residential condominiums. Over the years, **the Arcade** has served many uses. The ground floor seems to always have been reserved for shops, including prior to 1930 the Chautauqua Bookstore. Doctors' offices were on the 2nd floor and the 3rd floor housing the 500-seat Sherwood Recital Hall, named after piano instructor William H. Sherwood, was suc-

ceeded by a dormitory.

Ellis G. Hall of Jamestown, New York designed the Arcade. He was architect of many other Chautauqua projects including Alumnae Hall, the 1986 Pier Building, the Seaver Gym, and the Hall of Education. The scale of the building (occupying five lots), its multi-gabled roof and its natural color scheme make it a fitting border to the south side of Miller Park. The Arcade is listed in the National Register of Historic Places.

Photo by Selden Campen

Miller Park

During the Institution's first decade, Miller Park was the focal point of Chautauqua. At that time it was encircled by a double row of tents and small houses. The park was largely occupied by the "Auditorium" under a natural tree top roof with backless benches seating 2,000 people. Marking the site of the speaker's platform are the shrubs surrounding a chestnut stump encased in concrete and a dedication plaque. Narrow alleyways, close proximity of adjacent houses and the exposed plumbing, frequently seen in "old" Chautauqua, are not without risks. In the late 1880s fire destroyed the lakefront portion of the circle and those cottages were never rebuilt, providing the current lake vista. Some of the original tent platform houses remain on the north side of the park. The park was named for cofounder Lewis Miller after the Pavilion was built on the site of the current Amphitheater in 1887.

The Auditorium was the place where people came together to learn and to be entertained during the first five years.

The Auditorium – 1874 to 1878

Chautauqua archive photo

Photo by Selden Campen

Site of the "Auditorium's" speaker platform.

Photo by Selden Campen

Speaker's platform dedication plaque.

SITE OF
THE ORIGINAL PLATFORM
CHAUTAUQUA ASSEMBLY
1874

Photo by Selden Campen

Miller Cottage – 1875

Photo by Richard Campen

The Lewis **Miller Cottage** was completed in the summer of 1875 just in time to receive President Ulysses S. Grant. It is one of the very oldest and most interesting cottages on the grounds. Located at **28 Miller Park**, it is near the lake, facing the site of the first Auditorium at what is now Miller Park. One of the first prefabricated houses in America, it was constructed of lumber pre-cut in Lewis Miller's farm implement factory in Akron, Ohio, then shipped by train to Mayville and thence by steamboat to Fair Point.

Stylistically, the cottage suggests a Swiss Chalet, considered the most picturesque of all dwellings built of wood. Houses of this style are noted for their projecting roofs adapted to a snowy country, broad bracket-supported porches extending the width of the structure as well as rustic and quaint ornaments and detail. The walls of the Miller Cottage are one board in thickness with crisscross members serving as structural supports. It was more usual at the time to build with so-called "balloon-frame," introduced at mid-century (equal distance studs of pre-cut, sized dimensions). The Miller cottage is, therefore, of unique and in some respects advanced, design; it is certainly one of the earliest and oldest pre-fabricated structures extant in the United States. Originally, its ground floor contained a parlor and at least one, perhaps two, smaller rooms; the second floor was used as a dormitory for ladies. Early photographs show a boldly striped tent installed on an extension of the front porch that was used as a men's dormitory.

The Miller Cottage, designated a National Historic Landmark in 1966, has important and historic associa-

tions. Upon its completion President Grant became the first sitting president to visit Chautauqua. Cofounder John Heyl Vincent had been Grant's minister in Illinois. Thomas Alva Edison married Lewis Miller's daughter Mina, his second wife, and graduated from the CLSC in 1930. Mina was Miller's seventh of eleven children. The Edisons occupied the house sparodically, and were visited many times by their good friends Henry Ford and Harvey Firestone. President James A. Garfield was received there in 1880, when in an address at Palestine Park he said, "It has been the struggle of the world to gain more leisure, but it has been left to Chautauqua to show us how to use it." The Edison's son Charles, Governor of New Jersey and former Secretary of the Navy under President Franklin D. Roosevelt, was present when the cottage was designated a National Landmark in 1966.

In 1922 Mina Edison carried out extensive revisions and additions to the cottage, including a kitchen wing and bedroom. She remodeled the ground floor so the parlor now occupies the entire area. The former second floor ladies' dormitory was partitioned into separate bedrooms. She added the rear garden and caused two adjoining cottages to be demolished. At Chautauqua Mrs. Edison made outstanding contributions as an Institution trustee and president of the Bird, Tree and Garden Club. Mina Edison died in 1947 and ownership transferred to her niece, Nancy Arnn and, since 2010, to her son Ted Arnn and his wife Kim. In 2016 the Chautauqua Foundation, aided by a gift from Tom Hagan, purchased the Miller Cottage from the Arnn family.

Miller Park

View of Miller Park from the corner of Miller and Vincent looking east, with the site of the original speaker platform at the far left seen just above the head of the woman wearing a light blue shirt

Photo by Selden Campen

Dixie Cottage – Circa 1875

The **Dixie Cottage** was built on a preexisting tent platform at **5 Thompson Avenue**. Leaseholder Anna Ladd Dixey of New Orleans named her house as a play on her surname. Long owned by the Lucas family (1944-2010), the Dixie was recently purchased by Larry and Carol Rizzolo. It is a small Victorian one and one-half story white house with pink trim, Romanesque double doors and a gabled roof.

Photo by Carol Rizzolo

Alfred Landon Cottage

The **Alfred M. Landon Cottage** is at **20 Miller Park** at the left among the three tent platform cottages in close proximity to each other along the north side of Miller Park. It was built by Landon's grandfather, Reverend W. H. Mossman, in 1876. Alfred Landon was a Presidential nominee in 1936 running against Franklin D. Roosevelt. Landon's speech at Chautauqua drew 20,000, while FDR's "I Hate War" speech was attended by "only" 12,000.

Cottages on the north side of Miller Park

Photo by Selden Campen

Walker/Comay House – 1881

Built in 1881 of board and batten construction, the **Walker/Comay House** is at **11 North Lake Drive**. The left section of the house was added in the early 1900s. Mrs. H. E. Eddy willed the house to the Institution, after which it was used as a guesthouse for visiting clergy. Clark and Ethyl Reed of Midland, Pennsylvania bought the house from the Institution in 1959. It has since been inherited by the Elizabeth Reed and David Walker family, and the David and Gretchen Comay family.

In 1894 while the cellar was being excavated, a dozen or more Indian skeletons were found. Three of these are now in the Buffalo Museum of Science. Obed Edson's book, *History of Chautauqua County,* reports that the Erie tribe populated the Chautauqua region until the 17th century. It was then that Senecas of the Iroquois Federation destroyed the Eries in a savage attack. Fair Point is the possible site of an Indian burial ground.

Photo by Selden Campen

God's Country – 1880/1993

Photo by Selden Campen

Photo from the 1940s provided by Darlyne Johnston

God's Country Cottage at **1 North Lake Drive** dates back to 1880, four years after the first meeting of the Chautauqua Lake Sunday School Assembly. Before substantial renovation, this cottage was a fine example of a board and batten style construction, as seen at left.

Darlyne King Johnston now owns God's Country cottage; it has been in her family since 1964.

Sculptured tortoise relocated since this photo to the extension of Miller Park east of South Lake Dr.

Photo by Richard Campen

Children's Beach

Adjacent to the Pier Building are two of the four public beaches. The **Children's Beach** serves families with young children; the Institution provides life guards during the season at posted times.

Photo by Selden Campen

Miller Bell Tower – 1911

The Miller Bell Tower, designed by E.B. Green, was dedicated in 1911 as a memorial to cofounder Lewis Miller. Built largely of bricks, rising to its red tile roof at a height of sixty-nine feet, the sixteen square foot tower is supported by one hundred deep driven piles. In the general form of an Italian campanile, its open gallery contains fourteen bells, the largest weighing 3,033 pounds. The tower has come to be a symbol of Chautauqua as well as a landmark visible over great distances around the lakeshore. The land on which it stands is hallowed, in a sense, by the tens of thousands who for years arrived here at Fair Point. Carolyn Benton, the current bell ringer, welcomes visitors to her three fifteen-minute concerts at 8 a.m., 12 p.m. and 6 p.m. daily.

The tower's fourteen bells consist of the ten bells transferred from the original Pier Building plus four added in 1967. The Meneely Bell Foundry of Troy, New York cast the original ten bells, weighing in total 10,000 pounds, in 1885. Added were the 1878 Bryant Bell (used to celebrate the CLSC Bryant Day) and 3 new bells cast by the Petit & Fritzen Bell Foundry of the Netherlands. The larger bell choir affords the bell ringer to draw from an expanded musical repertoire. Additionally, in 1967 the bells were electrified and connected to a new console. Also, a new electric clock was installed and connected to the bells so that a Westminister chime rings on every quarter hour. The additional bells and the electrical clock were gifts of the Miller and Follansbee families, respectively.

Carolyn Benton plays the bell tower keyboard

Photo by Sellden Campen

Bryant Day Bellringer Tony Muir

Photo from The Chautauquan Daily – Ruby Wallau Staff Photographer

Pier Building – 1916

See photo on front cover.

Fair Point projects east into the lake just north of Palestine Park. At the Institution's founding and for the next quarter century, the main entrance to Chautauqua was via water. Fair Point provided a natural harbor for arriving boats, affording some protection from the frequent northwest winds.

Replacing an old dock that had become inadequate, the original 1886 Pier Building was a grand three-story structure with a tower housing ten bells that greeted the hourly arrival of steamboats. It was festive in appearance and contained ticketing and baggage offices on the first floor, shops and an observation veranda on the second, and dormitory and classrooms on the third.

By early 1900s most Chautauquans were arriving by the rail or auto at the road gate, and the pilings of the initial pier building had been damaged by the weight and motion of the bells, requiring frequent and costly repairs. The bells were moved to the new tower in 1911 and a new smaller pier building, designed by E.B. Green, was constructed in 1916.

Original Pier Building – Circa 1890

Photo from chautauquatrail.com

Current Pier Building

Photo by Richard Campen

Photo from my-travel-quotes.com

It houses the Pier Club, formerly the College Club, and some classrooms. The Club provides young adult Chautauquans (age 17 & up) Internet access, billiards, ping-pong, air hockey, a snack bar, a beach, TV lounge and frequent evening age-specific entertainment. In front of the Pier Building's colonnaded side is the College Beach and to its southwest is the Children's Beach, both open to the public.

Palestine Park – 1874

Do you see the mound of rocks at the far end of the park? Well, that is Mount Herman in the Holy Land. The rocks partially camouflage a fuel pump station used by the boat docks.

Palestine Park, originally 100 feet by 75 feet, was built of temporary materials along the lakefront south of Fair Point. Dr. W. W. Wyeth designed it in 1874 under commission from Bishop Vincent. Reconstructed, enlarged and remodeled several times over the next 14 years, it became similar to what we see today now having a length 350 feet (scale 1.75 feet per mile). Palestine Park is indeed a relief map of the Holy Land, albeit in the reverse direction, with the land contoured to indicate the low-lying Dead Sea in the southeast, Jordan River, Mount Herman in the north, and site markers for many of the more important biblical towns west thereof labeled Jericho, Jerusalem, Bethlehem, etc. used to retell the stories of both Old and New Testament. All the way from Dan to Beersheba, the Park represents the land of Israel and its surroundings.

The work of the Institution, in the words of John Heyl Vincent, was "normal training with the purpose of improving biblical instruction in the Sunday school and family." Children attending the boys' and girls' classes in those early years were taken on "pilgrimages" through Palestine Park.

Guided tours of Palestine Park are offered Sunday and Monday at 7 PM.

Biblical site markers

Rev. Noel Calhoun leading a Palestine Park tour.

Photo by Selden Campen

Hagen-Wensley Guest House – 1881/2011

At **22 South Lake Drive** on the northwest corner with Bowman Avenue is the **Hagen-Wensley Guest House**, restored in 2011. It provides attractive accommodations for speakers and performers visiting Chautauqua, privacy when they desire it and an immersion experience of what it is like being in residence in the Institution. The renovation, funded by the Hagans, included an improved foundation, an elevator, bathrooms within the guest rooms, a new kitchen and laundry, a new library and business center, and restored porches. News conferences with these celebrities are frequently held in the late morning on its comfortable porch overlooking Chautauqua Lake.

Built in the same year as the Athenaeum in 1881, it was a rooming house known as The Lafayette and later as The Windsor. President Arthur Bestor lived here dur-

ing his first three years at Chautauqua. It was acquired by Nina T. Wensley in 1952 and given by her in 1966 to the Institution, at which time the interior was remodeled and the building was renamed the Wensley House. Nina Wensley was an active Institution trustee for many years.

For 30 years through 2005 the affable Winnie Lewellen served as hostess at the house, followed by Rachel Borzilleri. The Hagan-Wensley House has accommodated guests as diverse as Barbara Bush, Bill Clinton, Fred Rogers and Betty Friedan. "The thing that brings so much joy to my heart is when people discover Chautauqua," Borzilleri said. "It really makes no difference if they are a Noble Peace Prize winner, or an accordionist or ventriloquist, or an ambassador. It's that all people who stay here walk away with a love of Chautauqua."

Photo by Selden Campen

33

Sports Club – 1942

In 1933, the **Sports Club**, an outgrowth of the lively Horseshoe Club, was organized as a recreation center for both men and women. The Club's activities expanded to include shuffleboard, lawn bowling, and boating (both manual and sail), as well as bridge and other games. Dating back to 1977, the premier event organized by the Sports Club has been the Old First Night Run, a fundraiser for the Institution.

The Sports Club occupies the site of the old electric powerhouse and pumping station. One year after its founding in 1902, the Men's Club moved into the building, which resembled an English castle with slit battlements along the roof perimeter and a 50-foot octagonal tower at one end. Inside, the club installed telephone, telegraph and stenographic services, a barbershop, showers, writing and smoking rooms and a reading room with metropolitan newspapers. The Men's Club served successfully as a meeting place for business and professional men until about 1930 when it was dissolved. In 1931 a new Yacht Club was formed and used the old clubhouse. Within another two years, the recently formed Sports Club shared the old castle with the yachtsmen. A new clubhouse was finally achieved in 1942 and the old powerhouse disappeared. The Yacht Club moved to new quarters at the south end of the grounds.

Photo by Selden Campen

At your mark, get set, . . .

Photo by Selden Campen

Mac-A-Tack
The Campen family's Macgregor 26', fifty horsepower sailboat was moored at the bouys off the Sports Club pier from 2000 to 2006.

Lawn Bowling – 1935

On the lawn in front and to the south of the Arcade is a lawn bowling green originally installed in 1935. Recently the green was totally rehabilitated: leveling, new turf, shelters, and fencing. Lawn bowling equipment can be rented at the Sports Club.

Photo by Selden Campen

Old First Night T-Shirts and Posters

Since about 1996, the Chautauqua Sports Club has retained Studio 4 East of Allegany, New York to prepare screen print T-shirts for participants and friends of the Old First Night race. Dan, Peter and Mikel Wintermantel (known as the Fabulous Shirtheads) at Studio 4 East have created fantastic designs for the Sports Club. Their art has become so popular that the Sports Club now offers them both as T-shirts and posters. Some Chautauquans collect this art in both forms as they may have collected baseball cards as children. For a number of years these designs were for sale as needlepoint canvases in Gretchen's Gallery at the Colonnade.

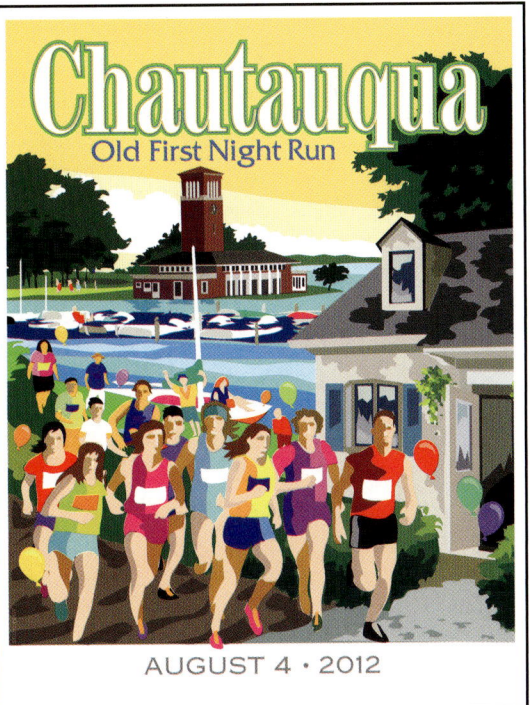

Athenaeum Hotel – 1881

Photo by Richard Campen

The **Athenaeum Hotel** at **26 South Lake Drive** was opened in 1881 just seven years after the founding of Chautauqua Institution. It is a large building originally having 200 rooms. The reduction of that number to 160 and the removal of an upper section of the central tower were results of subsequent renovations. Until recently the hotel operated on the American plan, three meals a day included in the daily rate; that now is an elective. It was built in 90 days at an original cost of $125,000 with funds provided by the founder Lewis Miller, his brother Jacob Miller, and Clement Studebaker, successful carriage (then automobile) manufacturer. That the Athenaeum was among the very earliest buildings anywhere to be lighted by electricity is sometimes attributed to Thomas A. Edison's connection with Chautauqua; he had installed electricity in his father-in-law's house (the Lewis Miller Cottage) as early as 1879.

The "Grand Dame" of Chautauqua

Chautauqua Archive photo

The traditional entrance to the building is at the north end, where a large L-shaped entry lobby runs south to the reservation desk at its corner and then east to the grand veranda facing the lake. The east-west portion of the corridor is flanked on the north by a spacious lounge, 35 feet by 75 feet, furnished entirely with old wicker, and to the south by a dining room, 58 feet by 75 feet, seating 300 persons. These rooms have trussed ceilings, eliminating the usual obstructive columns. A. K. Warren, Superintendent of Grounds and Buildings, carried out its advanced design. A roof supported by dozens of 30-foot high columns shelters the veranda.

Originally the 145-foot tower contained an additional Mansard element, above that now existing, which included a spacious suite. Commencing in 1982, an extensive restoration was undertaken; the principal public rooms were refurbished, the porch was extended with roomy polygonal elements at either end and the exterior painted with a combination of Victorian colors. In 1983 Robert C. Gaede, architect of the project, installed the curving dual staircase providing access from the veranda to the spacious front lawn and the lake. This has as its centerpiece a cast iron fountain. The Athenaeum is something to behold!

The news release at the time the Athenaeum was completed in 1881 said: "There is no modern appointment lacking in this great structure. The first class barber shop, the telegraph office, the telephone office, electric bells, gas and electric lights, hot and cold baths, magnificent parlors, large rooms – well lighted and ventilated, elevators, music – everything to make it most complete. The table is such to tempt the appetite, the servants are attentive, the guests cultured, the proprietor genial and gentlemanly, and the terms moderate."

An annex was added to the hotel in 1924 and a new elevator installed. The second floor passageway between the annex and the main structure forms an intriguing archway over Janes Avenue.

Preceding the Athenaeum was the Palace Hotel, a half-tent, half-framed structure that had been first used at the 1876 Centennial Exposition in Philadelphia, and moved to Chautauqua a year later. By 1880, Lewis Miller and others decided Chautauqua needed a first-rate hotel and organized a stock company to construct the Athenaeum.

The Athenaeum Hotel is available for stays of a night, a week or the entire summer season. The hotel hosts conferences, weddings, and other events in the off-season and is closed November through April. In October 1996, it became a temporary White House when President Bill Clinton arrived with his staff to prepare for the presidential debates.

Painting by Jerome Chesley

Clinton Entourage and Athenaeum Hotel Staff – October, 1996

Chautauqua Archive photo

The Women's Club – 1929

Photo by Gena Bedrosian

The clubhouse of the **Chautauqua Women's Club** (CWC) at **30 South Lake Drive** is immediately identifiable by its gracious tall-columned portico. F.J. Kidd and W.A. Kidd, architects from Buffalo, designed the clubhouse in the Georgian style. It was built in 1929, the year of the great stock market crash, on the former site of Jacob Miller's flamboyant Victorian cottage (see inset next page). Lewis Miller's brother, Jacob, had built that house circa 1880. The front room of the current clubhouse is a spacious, attractively furnished parlor extending the entire width of the building. In the rear is a well-appointed dining room to the right and a kitchen to the left. Upstairs are single rooms available to rent. On the 50th anniversary of the clubhouse it was added to the National Register of Historic Places. In 2010 CWC undertook a major remodeling project at a cost of $450,000. Both floors were made accessible to the handicapped (including installation of an elevator),

new furnishings were purchased and the 1880 Steinway grand piano in the parlor was restored.

Women began meeting at Chautauqua in 1874 at a time when men's and women's groups met separately. But it was not until fifteen years later that Chautauqua Institution recognized the women's group, when in 1889 the CWC was organized. The original dues for the season were 25 cents. Early on, national women speakers at the CWC included Emily Huntington Miller (author and sister-in-law to Lewis Miller), Francis Willard (second president of the WCTU), Emma P. Ewing (home economics author and educator) and Mary A. Livermore (temperance and prison reformer). Many other prominent Americans have visited the clubhouse; recently among them is Justice Sandra Day O'Connor.

The CWC is extremely active in sponsoring lectures, social events and money-raising activities for the benefit of Chautauqua. The most well known of its past presidents was Anna J. Hardwicke Pennybacker, who previously had led the General Federation of Women's Clubs from 1915 to 1917. That influential national group had a membership of about 400,000 women. Mrs. Pennybacker assumed office in 1917 and served for twenty-one years. Under her leadership the CWC purchased the Jacob Miller cottage and in three years (with many women turning in WW I war bonds to realize the goal) paid off the mortgage on this initial clubhouse. Within a decade the CWC expanded beyond expectations and required a larger facility for carrying out its mission, and the present building was constructed.

Eleanor Roosevelt, following one of her several visits to Chautauqua between 1927 and 1937, was granted life membership status in the CWC. In response Mrs. Roosevelt invited the entire CWC to visit the White House on January 21, 1935. She and her staff were surprised when 903 women arrived, so a buffet lunch was offered. Chautauqua President Arthur Bestor was the only man who attended the event. At the end of 1934 the CWC had about 1,700 members.

The CWC welcomes men and accepts them into membership, even leadership positions, except for its presidency. The Club prides itself in the number of young artists (vocal, instrumental, dance, theatrical, and visual) that it is able to support through scholarships to the Chautauqua Summer Schools of Fine and Performing Arts – annually between $80,000 and $100,000, assisting more than 60 student artists.

Photo by Robert Cahn

Principal activities of the CWC are the Contemporary Issues Forum (Saturday afternoon lectures by nationally prominent speakers), Chautauqua Speaks (presentations by Chautauquans on Thursday mornings) and Bridge at the Clubhouse (twice weekly). In 2009 the CWC started a group to network Chautauqua professional women. Its major fund-raisers are the Flea Boutique (resale of donated goods), Strawberry Festival and Arts at the Market (sale of crafts and art created by local Chautauquans). There are many other activities too numerous to mention.

Photo by Robert Cahn

32 South Lake – WCTU Headquarters – before 1885

Photo by Richard Campen

Although now a private family residence, from 1924 through 1946, **32 South Lake Drive** was the **Woman's Christian Temperance Union** (WCTU) Headquarters. Many believe this High-Victorian Cottage to be the most beautiful and interesting house in Chautauqua. Pictured here is the house in the mid-1980s when it was dressed in a stunning blue awning.

At the time it was built (prior to 1885), some believed that germs and evil spirits resided in the 90-degree corners of rooms. The Octagon building near Alumnae Hall and 32 South Lake Drive are examples where the architects' designs eliminated or reduced the number of such corners. The gables in this house, its tower, its decorative barge boards and paired columns furnish an example of American folk art in Chautauqua Homes.

The earliest records available show that Mr. & Mrs. John S. Rogers owned 32 South Lake Drive in 1885. The Chess family sold it to the WCTU in 1924 on the 50th anniversary of the WCTU's founding. The James G. Haller family purchased it from the organization in 1946. There have been several subsequent transfers.

Prior to 1924, the WCTU was headquartered in the first floor of Kellogg Hall. Upon purchase of 32 South Lake Drive, the stained glass Francis Willard Memorial Window was moved from Kellogg Hall and installed in 32 South Lake. When the WCTU moved its headquarters to Chicago in 1946, the memorial window was moved once again.

It may not be well-known that the formation of the WCTU in November 1874 resulted from a meeting of women held at Fair Point during the first Sunday School Assembly. The Chautauqua Meeting took place after a vigorous and prayerful campaign against the sale of liquor occurred in Ohio and Western New York. Hundreds of women had been drawn into the crusade. Mrs. Emily Miller, Secretary of the Chautauqua Meeting (later first President of the Chautauqua Women's Club), signed the call for a convention in Cleveland in November for the purpose of uniting the efforts of women in all states in the cause of temperance. At the convention, the WCTU was formed and Francis Willard became its first president. In 1876 Francis Willard became the first woman to speak on the Chautauqua platform. At 32 years of age she became president of Evanston College for Ladies, which later merged with Northwestern University. She resigned from the college to take on the presidency of the WCTU, leaving academic life to enroll in the temperance army. She died in 1898.

At the 1874 organizing convention of the National WCTU, the members were urged to erect drinking fountains in their home towns so that men could get a drink of water without entering saloons. Many of the fountains erected by Local WCTUs are still in existence; some still give water and a number have been restored.

Other Distinguished Homes on South Lake Drive

Photos on this page by Selden Camen

United Methodist Missionary Home – 1903

The **United Methodist Missionary Home** at **34 South Lake Drive** was built in 1903 as the summer residence for Anna Carlisle, daughter of Clement Studebaker, carriage and automobile manufacture. For a brief period in 1899, Studebaker was president of the Institution after Lewis Miller died. The building stands out on the lakeshore for its considerable mass and barn-red color contrasting with the white trim. Inside, one is in the world of the Arts & Crafts movement – a turning away from Victorian frills in favor of hand-crafted, utilitarian design that was coming into vogue when the cottage was built.

Hukill-Lacey Cottage – Before 1880

Fanciful Victorian fretwork originally swathed the **Hukill-Lacey Cottage** at **38 South Lake Drive.** Its scrollwork and wood-lace were removed in 1901. The home remained in the Hukill-Lacey family for close to a century.

Neubauer Cottage – 1881

The **Neubauer Cottage** at **42 South Lake Drive** was built in 1881 as a duplex by Frank W. Higgins, later governor of New York. He and his sister, together funded Higgins Hall (now the Chautauqua Cinema). The cottage was stripped of its Victorian garb in the 1930s. The Neubauer/Rolley/Talpas family acquired it in 1962. Joseph Neubauer was president of PPG from 1967 to 1976 and an Institution trustee from 1976 to 1984.

McKee Karslake Cottage – Circa 1896

The **McKee Karslake Cottage** at **44 South Lake Drive** was built circa 1896. The interesting two-story, wrap-around verandas are recessed under a roof supported by fluted Ionic columns, perhaps resulting from concurrent Grecian travels by the builder. Inside are three impressive fireplaces, each with a mantel resting on turned, freestanding Ionic columns in different woods, framing attractive tile insets. The Karslakes have owned the cottage since 1950.

Bishop's Garden – 1940

Founder Dr. John Heyl Vincent's cottage, located just to the south of the Missionary Home at **36 South Lake Drive**, burned to the ground in 1901. The **Bishop's Garden**, a memorial to him created in 1940, now occupies the site. Its centerpiece is a circular pool presided over by a nude little boy with outstretched arms sculpted by Ruth Sherwood, daughter of Professor William H. Sherwood of Chicago, who for years headed Chautauqua School of Music Piano department.

The backdrop in this photograph of the fountain is the **Baird-Wineman Cottage** (late 1870s) at **5 Peck**. A riot of color in addition to the scroll-saw work exemplifies the exuberance and gaiety of the Carpenter Gothic style.

Photo by Selden Campen

Youth Activities Area

Chautauqua's Boys' and Girls' Clubs are the oldest day camps in the U.S. (1893/95)

Chautauqua Institution has invested considerably, both in land and structures, to provide programming for children. Starting in 1878, classes for children were held in the Children's Temple located on what is now Bestor Plaza. Eight years later, in 1886, Dr. William G. Anderson founded The School of Physical Education that provided gymnastics courses for all ages. In their book, *Chautauqua Boys' and Girls' Club*, Rebecca Habenicht and Gratia Maley wrote "In 1893, Dr. William G. Anderson and Dr. James A. Babbitt envisioned

a permanent department of the Chautauqua Institution where boys could gather in one area so friendships could be solidified and they could develop their physical well-being while supplementing their schoolwork and moral training . . . their plan came to fruition on August 14, 1893 when the Boys' Club began its inaugural two-week session. The first summer was such a success, the Boys' Club has met the entire summer ever since." In 1895 the Girls' Club, founded by Miss Helen Bainbridge, initially offered activities in cooking, singing, rowing and bathing (swimming), supplemented by classes in nature and various entertainments.

The Youth Activities Area occupies the lake-level plain extending south from Park Avenue to the Institution perimeter at Bryant Street. Along the lake shore east of South Lake Drive from north to south are Heinz Beach, the Youth Activities Center (also known as the "YAC"), the Club sailboat dock, Seaver Gym, volleyball courts, Boys' Club, the Beeson Youth Center, an extensive swimming area divided into sections and enclosed with piers, and soccer/activity fields. West of South Lake Drive are the Girls' Club, Sharpe Field, a playground and tennis and basketball courts.

Painting by Robin K Robins — rkrobins@hotmail.com

Youth Activities Center and Heinz Beach – 1916

At the entry to the youth area at the south end of the grounds is a building which houses the Heinz Beach Bathhouse and Fitness Center on the lower level facing the lake and the Youth Activities Center on the upper level with entry on the opposite side. This building, dating back to 1916, was originally the Bolin Gym. The 2nd floor gym became the summer home of the Columbus Boys Choir from 1944 to 1957, then housed the Chautauqua School of Dance, and since 1981, the Youth Activities Center. YAC is a gathering place where youth and early teens can get a snack or meal, socialize, watch TV and play ping-pong or pool. Others can also buy lunch there. The YAC's popularity is evidenced by the collection of bikes near the entrance and surrounding pathways when it is open.

Heinz Beach Bath House & Fitness Center on lower level pictured before its 2002 renovation.

Photo by Selden Campen

Youth Activities Center Porch on second floor of YAC and Heinz Beach House Building.

Photo from The Chautauquan Daily – Ruby Wallau Staff Photographer

Living up to its name, the YAC holds events every night for kids – "Make Your Own Sundae" night, dance night, wing night and other fun activities. In addition, YAC has ping-pong tables, pool tables and space to just hang around with friends.

Youth Activities Center upper level.

Photo by Selden Campen

Girls' Club – 1902

The **Girls' Club** at **60 South Lake Drive** serves as an organizational meeting place at the beginning of each camp day. The large open floor plan surrounded by porches on the first floor provides ample breakout space for campers of different ages and a place for indoor rainy day activities and guest speakers. On the second floor is dormitory space where some counselors who are without family homes on the Institution grounds reside. Girls' Club meets from 9 to 12 in the mornings and 2 to 4 in the afternoon.

Photo by Selden Campen

Beside the Girls' Club is a flat play area sporting a wigwam for creative play. Along the south perimeter of this space is a creek descending from the ravine to the lake. Filled with fossils, easy to find by uncovering a layer of shale rock, makes this an attractive place for campers to share time with one another.

Photo by Selden Campen

Photo by Robert Cahn

Sharpe Field Grandstand – 1911, Rebuilt – 1991

Baseball was a major spectator sport at Chautauqua. The "Chautauqua Nine," founded in 1888 under the leadership of Alonzo Stagg, one of Yale's top athletes, drew large crowds. Baseball also thrived under the leadership of Albert Sharpe in whose honor the field is named. A smaller metal grandstand was built in 1991 after the original 1911 grandstand was destroyed in a raging fire ignited by a careless youth playing with fireworks under the then wooden bleachers. Softball replaced hardball as the game of choice in the 1960s. Both men's and women's softball competitions are sponsored by the Chautauqua Sports Club in a near season-long series.

Photo by Selden Campen

Photo from The Chautauquan Daily – Ruby Wallau / Staff Photographer

With her eye on the ball and a smile on her face, **Catherine McFarland,** from Merion Station, Pennsylvania bats during the fourth annual mother-daughter softball game at Sharpe Field on Sunday, July 19, 2015. Catherine is a 3rd generation Chautauquan, having spent every summer of her life at the Institution. Like many other Chautauquans she attended the Chautauqua Children's School for 4 summers before becoming a Girls' Club camper for the following 9 summers. Catherine plays in the Chautauqua softball league on the Chautauqua Lakers team.

Seaver Gymnasium – 1890/2000

Seaver Gym, built in 1889 to house an active gymnastics program, was named after Dr. George Seaver who was prominent in the development of the Physical Education Department. Renovations to the gymnasium in 2000 included new basketball backboards and rims, refinished walls, improved balcony, upgrades in electricity and plumbing, increased capacity in the bathrooms and a new walkway entrance to the basketball court, which occupies the second floor and is surrounded by a third floor balcony. The locker room on the lower level is used by the Boys' Club.

Pre-renovation photo by Selden Campen

Photo by Selden Campen

Boys' Club -1899/2000

Built in 1899, five years after the club's first full season, the **Boys' Club** houses the oldest day camp in the nation. The camp serves boys ages 7 through 15 with a program of field, water, craft, nature and music activities. Camp meets from 9 to 12 in the morning and 2 to 4 in the afternoon, providing constructive play and development time for children and teens, while affording their parents time to attend lectures and/or participate in other activities.

Camp life, however, need not stop at age 15. Teens may move directly from camp to the Counselor-In-Training (CIT) Program, where they are instructed in teaching strategies, first aid, handling challenging situations, and creating one-of-a-kind games. Many senior counselors come from the ranks of campers who subsequently attended the CIT program.

Photo by Selden Campen

Volleyball courts between Seaver Gym (out of sight on the left) and Boys' Club on the right.

Photo by Selden Campen

Boys' and Girls' Club large swimming area behind the Beeson Youth Center.

Painting by Robin K Robins — rkrobins@hotmail.com

Beeson Youth Center – 1968

Atheletic Club photo from the Chautauqua Archive Postcard Collection

The **Beeson Youth Center** is on the lake front below Sharpe Memorial Field and was built in 1968 as a memorial to Charles and Ruth Anne Beeson. The building houses the Boys' and Girls' Club headquarters, staff apartments and rooms, and provides space for indoor games and crafts. Mr. Beeson was a member of the Institution's Board of Trustees. The building replaced the **Athletic Club,** erected in 1905, which provided space for storage of members rowing shells and small boats, four bowling alleys and lounge areas.

Photo by Selden Campen

Sample Cottage & Beach House

The beach house between the Beeson Youth Center and the sports field along the lake belongs to the Sample family. They also own a house on the hill at **14 Emerson** above the ball field with stonework to match. It is the only private property along the shoreline south of South Avenue. Both Paul Sample and his wife Helen Heinz Sample served on the Institution's Board of Trustees.

Photo by Selden Campen

Photo by Selden Campen

Coyle Tennis Courts, Playground, & The Lake

Photo by Selden Campen

Photo by Jeanne Wiebenga

Chautauqua Belle

Photo by Robert Cahn

Chautauqua Lake, at 1,308 feet above sea level, is one of the highest navigable waters in North America. It offers exceptional fishing for walleye, bass, muskellunge and several species of pan fish.

Located in the southeast corner of Chautauqua County, Chautauqua Lake is about 17.5 miles long and has a surface area of 13,156 acres.

The lake is divided at Bemus Point into two basins of nearly equal size. The north basin of Chautauqua Lake is on average 25 feet deep with a maximum depth of 75 feet. The south basin is considerably shallower, with an average depth of 11 feet and a maximum depth of 19 feet.

The water from the lake drains to the south, emptying first into the Chadakoin River in Jamestown, New York, before traveling east into Conewango Creek. The creek flows south, entering the Allegheny River in Warren, Pennsylvania and this flows into the Ohio River in Pittsburgh, which drains into the Mississippi River.

The Chautauqua Lake Watershed has likely been inhabited for 10,000 to 12,000 years. The first significant impacts to the lake and watershed, however, did not occur until the 19th century, when deforestation and overfishing were at their peak. Warner Dam was built in 1919 and is currently used to partially regulate lake levels. Chautauqua Lake has a long history of water quality monitoring. The lake was first sampled by the New York State Conservation Department as early as 1937.

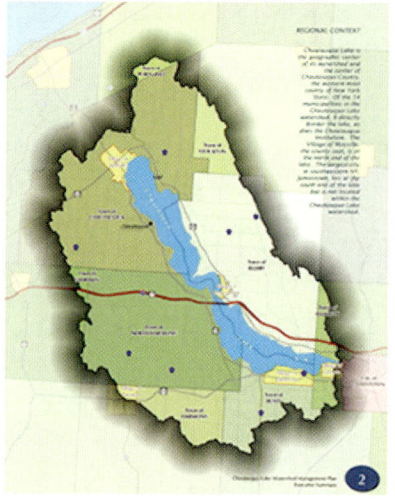

Figure from the Chautauqua Lake Watershed Management Plan

John R. Turney Sailing Center – 2006

Photo by Selden Campen

Jean and Dick Turney established the **John R. Turney Sailing Center** in memory of their son. The center was built around the original beams and concrete floor of the Coyle Pavilion (1993) that was merged with newly built knotty pine walls to create a facility with two classrooms. The sailing center includes numerous sailboats (principally Sunfish, Optimists, International 420s and Flying Scots) chosen for their suitability in teaching young sailors. It includes docks, classrooms, launching crane and ramp and a repair/storage shed. The center provides instruction to sailors and would-be sailors of all ages, sailboat rentals and is home to the Chautauqua Yacht Club, which hosts the area's most competitive regattas.

Prior to the sailing center's existence, a small-scale sailing program for the Boys' and Girls' Club provided instruction to campers; additionally there were small boat rentals at the Sports Club. The Turney Sailing Center has greatly broadened sailing opportunities at Chautauqua. The funding it earns allows for a vastly improved boat maintenance program than previously existed. Few places with such sailing facilities and instruction are available today for families.

Chautauqua Optimist Fleet.

Turner Sailing Center class enrollment and sailboat rental office.

Photo from The Chautauquan Daily – Saalik Khan Staff Photographer

Photo by Selden Campen

Chautauqua Utitity District
Wastewater Treatment Plant – 1893/1978

The Chautauqua Utility District (CUD) treats sewage at its **Wastewater Treatment Plant** on Bryant Avenue at the south end of the grounds, adjacent to the Turney Sailing Center. It's a complicated and expensive process. In 1893 Chautauqua became the first completely sewered community in the U.S. Some of the tanks installed in the 1890 era remained in service for nearly 100 years, until a new plant came on line in 1978.

The plant uses a multi-stage process of cleaning "influent" to a level below EPA and New York state-mandated standards before the "effluent" is permitted to enter the lake. This involves clarifying tanks and rotating contactors. The Wastewater Treatment Plant has the capacity to process 840,000 gallons of influent daily. An average daily flow during the season is around 500,000 gallons – off-season around 50,000 gallons. Following filtration, the solid and sedimentary matter is hauled to Jamestown where it undergoes further treatment prior to being deposited in the county landfill.

CUD maintains another facility, a Water Filtration Plant, behind the Colonnade; however, its principal office is at the Wastewater Treatment Plant. Also at the Wastewater Treatment Plant is a well-equipped lab for testing water at various stages of its cleaning process. CUD maintains a staff of nine part- and full-time employees reporting through a superintendent to a board of five CUD commissioners serving three-year renewable terms. Commissioners must be residents and owners of taxable real estate in the district as well as Chautauqua town voters.

Primary and secondary clarifiers at the Chautauqua Wastewater Treatment Facility

Photo from The Chautauquan Daily – Saalik Khan Staff Photographer

Photo from The Chautauquan Daily – Eve Edelheit Staff Photographer

Core team at the Chautauqua Utility District pictured (left to right) are Gordy Pugh, CUD Superintendant Tom Cherry, Don Constantino, Karen McCann, Steve Spas and Mike Starks.

Photo from The Chautauquan Daily – Eve Edelheit Staff Photographer

Jones-Copeland Cottage

Photo by Selden Campen

Unique for its enclosed widow's walk, a platform from which, it is said, a sailor's wife could watch for her husband's anticipated return from sea, the **Jones-Copeland Cottage** is located at **20 Whittier Avenue**. The Jones family was reported to have said the house was patterned after a small villa seen in Italy. Architectural historian Richard Campen refers to the home as a British Colonial – a one and one-half story block surrounded on two or more sides with a veranda. This house is well suited for Chautauquans' favorite pastime of reading on the porch while watching pedestrians walk by.

Fenton Methodist Deaconess Home – 1917

The **Fenton Methodist Deaconess Home** at **21 Hawthorne Avenue** was built by the Methodist Episcopal Church as a residence for the deaconesses at Chautauqua. It offers six single rooms and one double room for deaconesses and home missionaries at no charge; their family and guests are accommodated for a donation. Located on the corner of Hawthorne and Wythe Avenues, the house was dedicated in 1917 as a memorial to the wife of James Fenton, a Buffalo industrialist. According to an agreement with Chautauqua Institution, Mr. Fenton provided that deaconesses of the United Methodist Church do not pay a gate fee.

Photo by Selden Campen

Thunder Bridge – 1900/1988

Photo by Selden Campen

Thunder Bridge reopened on June 28, 1988. "Let's hear the thunder," said James Copeland, Vice Chairman of the Board of Trustees, as he invited some 100 people to walk across Thunder Bridge. The bridge is more than just a connection between one part of the grounds and another. It is a tradition. When bicycles are ridden over the bridge, a sound similar to thunder can be heard throughout the ravine it spans. The thunder is part of the ambiance of Chautauqua.

Built to accommodate horse and carriage as well as foot traffic, the original Thunder Bridge was completed in 1900. Prior to its construction there had been no through streets on the southern part of the grounds. When Thunder Bridge was completed Chautauquans could circle the entire grounds for the first time.

The new bridge was built in Pittsburgh by Industrial Steel, arriving at Chautauqua in three sections. When the old structure was demolished, the four end posts were saved. They have now been installed at the ends of the new bridge, adding a touch of authenticity and sentimentality.

ELI CHENG

Photo by Jackie Campen

Bird, Tree & Garden Club Outdoor Classrooms

The **Bird, Tree and Garden Club** (BTG) constructed the outdoor classrooms under the direction of Bill Mealy, who was a mentee of Gilbert Burgeson before taking over the Chautauqua Naturalist position. This position as well as the outdoor classrooms and all BTG programming has always been funded by BTG with no expense to the Institution. The BTG also maintains the Arboretum on Wythe at the south end of the grounds, a gift from Henrietta Ord Jones, and the Butterfly Garden on Massey near the entrance to the South Parking Lot. Its headquarters are at Smith Wilkes Hall off Fletcher between Janes and Foster Avenues.

The **Roger Tory Peterson Outdoor Classroom**, built in 1999, is located in the ravine behind the Hall of Christ. The Bird, Tree and Garden Club uses it for a wide variety of storytelling programs. Roger Tory Peterson (1908-1996) of Jamestown, New York was a world-class educator, naturalist, author, photographer, ornithologist, conservationist and "Friend of the Chautauqua Institution." He is most widely noted for his extensive series of nature guides. The Roger Tory Peterson Institute, at 311 Curtis Street near the Jamestown Community College, is well worth a visit during your stay in Western New York.

Terry Mosher, nature consultant, speaking about birds and nature at the Roger Tory Peterson Classroom

Photo from The Chautauquan Daily – Caitkin Prarat Staff Photographer

Photo from The Chautauquan Daily – Greg Funka Staff Photographer

The **Mabel Powers Fire Circle,** built in 1999, is located by walking up the path along the creek up the ravine from Girls' Club. Mabel Powers (1872-1966) was well known at Chautauqua and elsewhere for her lectures and stories of the Iroquois. In recent years, Paul Leone, author and historian, has been a frequent speaker at the Bird, Tree and Garden Club's Native American Storytelling program.

The **Burgeson Nature Classroom**, built in 1996, is located in the ravine off Fletcher near the Girls' Club. It is where nature talks are normally held. O. Gilbert Burgeson was the Chautauqua Institution's naturalist for 37 years. At the Classroom's dedication in honor of the then 98 year old Mr. Burgeson, Bill Mealy led over 100 Chautauquans in singing "For He's a Jolly Good Fellow."

Bruce Robinson delivers a "Tree Talk" at the Burgeson Outdoor Classroom.

Photo by Michael Gelfield

Photo from The Chautauquan Daily – Caitlin Prarat Staff Photographer

Hall of Christ – 1909/1967

Photo by Selden Campen

The Hall of Christ is an off-white, brick, terra cotta and stone building with a grand classical portico supported by four Ionic columns. Paul J. Pelz, designer of the Library of Congress building, was the architect. The entrance to the building is by a set of stairs, raising the portico to a level that gives dignity to the building and a view of the surrounding area. Two 1,000-pound cornerstones were laid on August 7, 1900 containing a Bible, photos of founders Lewis Miller and John Vincent, a Lafayette dollar and a daily newspaper. The pediment over the 4 columns depicts the Bible with "arms" disseminating its message in all directions. The niches on either side of the door were intended to bear sculptured figures.

Inside, the 250-seat auditorium has many uses. During the summer these include a Roman Catholic mass on Sunday mornings, overflow and rainy day seating for Hall of Philosophy programs (via contemporaneous video transmission), Archives Department programs, CLSC Science Group lectures and Eventide Travel Series presentations. It is also a year-round center for conferences and receptions. Housed inside the Hall of Christ are the historically interesting Gould Bible Collection and the Tallman Tracker organ.

The Tallman organ, mounted on the dais at the front of the upper level meeting room, is a mechanical instrument. This means there is a mechanical linkage between each key or pedal pressed by the organist and the trackers, or valves, that allow air to be released from the organ's pipes thereby producing sound. It was constructed in 1893 for the First Baptist Church in Nyack, New York and moved to the Hall of Christ in 2000.

Gifts from Mrs. Robert D. Campbell and the Gebbie Foundation in 1967 made possible renovation of the lower level to include two large meeting rooms, a kitchenette and rest rooms as well as new interior furnishings upstairs.

Stan Toops pumps air into the Tallman Organ

Photo from The Chautauquan Daily – Roxana Pop Staff Photographer

Episcopal Chapel Of The Good Shepherd – 1894

The **Episcopal Chapel of the Good Shepherd**, located at the corner of Clark and Park Avenues, was completed in 1894. Administered by St. Paul's Episcopal Church in Mayville, it seats 150 people. This Carpenter Gothic style miniature church is used for services during the season and for weddings off-season. The veranda in front of this jewel of a building goes up to a peak topped by a cross. The bright red iron-hinged doors are festive. The building boasts a shingled roof and an unusual projecting bell hood. Cathedral stained glass windows light the interior and the white painted exterior is set off by surrounding greenery. An exterior wheelchair lift on the right side of the Chapel was added in 2004.

Painting by Jerome Chesley

Chapel of the Good Shepherd Interior.

Photo by Selden Campen

Chapel of the Good Shepherd in early 1900s.

Photo from Story of Chautauqua by Jesse Hurlbut

HALL OF PHILOSOPHY – 1879/1906

The **Hall of Philosophy** (HOP) has been called the second most important building on the grounds – second only to the Amphitheater. It also is among the most photogenic. Begun in 1903 and completed in 1906, architect E.B. Green has provided an exceedingly useful, practical and beautiful open-air auditorium – it is so well planned, so well situated and so appropriate to the programs held there. In this day and age when most lectures and symposia are conducted indoors, this open-air pavilion at Chautauqua is novel.

The dark brown stained roof timbers contrast dramatically with the 16 large Doric white fluted columns. Four trusses supporting extended eaves aid somewhat in protecting those assembled from sun and adverse weather. In the floor are mosaic tablets in honor of the CLSC classes that had contributed toward the building. Four-foot high masonry pedestals outside each corner of the Hall bear classical caldrons supported by tripods – a gift of one or more CLSC classes. Interior seating is approximately 800.

The **Hall in the Grove**, predecessor of the Hall of Philosophy, was a similar temple but with square columns. Built in 1879, in St. Paul's Grove, it is somewhat surprising that the Greek temple model was chosen. The nation's infatuation with "things Greek" had largely spent itself by the early 1850s in favor of Tuscan, Gothic and Romanesque revival styles. However, in this case the Greek style of the Hall of Philosophy seems quite appropriate.

Hall Of Philosophy – 1906

Painting by Mary Ann Boysen — art@maboysen.com — www.maboysen.com

Hall in the Grove – 1879

Photo from Story of Chautauqua by Jesse Hurlbut

HOP Floor Mosaic

Photo by Richard Campen

HOP Cauldron

Photo by Richard Campen

Pictorial Guide to Chautauqua

Hall of Philosophy ("HOP") as seen looking up the hill from Fletcher Avenue.

Photo by Robert Cahn

Hall Of Philosophy – Religious Studies Classroom

Photo by Jeanne Wiebenga

Photo by Selden Campen

HOP – CLSC Graduation Auditorium

HOP – Wedding Sanctuary (Ross Oliver escorts his daughter Carrie into the Hall of Philosophy)

Photo from The Chautauquan Daily – Photographer Unknown

Photo by Selden Campen

Williamsburg characters George Washington and Thomas Jefferson address party politics, taxes and power of the people in the Hall of Philosophy – August 24, 2011

Photo by Selden Campen

"Keeper of the Gate" unlocks the entrance to the Hall of Philosophy – Gate donated by the Class of 2000.

Photo from The Chautauquan Daily – Ruby Wallau Staff Photographer

Andrew Campen, Michael Minor and Kyle Oliver carry CLSC banners in the Recognition Day Parade

Photo by Selden Campen

Hall Of Missions – 1924

Photo by Selden Campen

A bronze sculpture of St Francis, a gift of the Globe Club in 1933, is on the Clark Avenue side of the hall. The statue is the work of Ruth Sherwood, daughter of William H. Sherwood, first Head of the Chautauqua School of Music Piano Department.

St. Francis and the Wolf of Gubbio

Photo by Jeanne Wiebenga

The **Hall of Missions** at **32 Cookman Avenue** between Wythe and Clark was built in 1924 to serve as headquarters for Chautauqua's Department of Religion. Its architect was Franklyn Kidd. During the season it is the residence of the Director of the Department of Religion as well as the weekly chaplains who conduct devotional services in the Amphitheater, and the afternoon religion lecturers who speak at the Hall of Philosophy.

In addition to apartments, the building contains a conference room, classroom, and parlor. The front porch provides a space for discussion and seating for those seeking comfort rather than proximity to the Hall of Philosophy lectures. The classroom is used by the Unity denomination for Sunday morning services.

The CLSC Class of 1884's building was razed to make way for the Hall of Missions.

Octagon Building – 1885

Built in 1885 by Pittsburgh CLSC members, the **Octagon Building** at **34 Cookman Avenue** was acquired by the CLSC classes of 1883-1886 four years later and brought to Chautauqua as a meeting room. Its walls are 8 feet wide on all sides. Outfitted as a one-room schoolhouse, it has been used for the writer's workshops, art appreciation, chess and other classes. Additionally, the Society of Friends (Quakers) use the Octagon Building for Sunday morning services.

Photo by Richard Campen

Painting by Robin K Robins – rkrobins@hotmail.com

Pioneer Hall – 1885

Photo by Selden Campen

Pioneer Hall (before 1921)

Photo from Story of Chautauqua by Jesse Hurlbut

Located at **36 Cookman Avenue, Pioneer Hall** was built in 1885 as a gathering place by the first class to graduate (in 1882) from the Chautauqua Literary and Scientific Circle. Members called themselves "The Pioneers." It is of Gothic Revival style with a gable in front of a higher gable as a roof. Spindle sawn art spans between columns with gingerbread in the corners.

Now a museum, the building contains many mementoes of early Chautauqua. On display is the pulpit used by Bishop John Vincent. The hall is lit only by candlelight and kerosene lamps. Over the years, formal maintenance responsibilities have transferred to the Class of 1938 and more recently to the Class of 1963.

In comparing the photo above and below, it appears Pioneer Hall has been raised approximately one and one-half feet and a staircase added to the front center subsequent to its original construction. Except for shingles, the building was painted only in white until recent times. *Chautauqua Impressions,* published in 1984, showed the hall painted white rather than red.

CLSC Banners

Since its inception, the Chautauqua Literary and Scientific Circle classes have elected a class president, written a class chant, selected a class motto and created a class banner. The class banner is used in the Parade of the Classes, held in the morning of Recognition Day (graduation day), to delineate the start of each class. Chautauquans have come to treasure these banners.

In 2011 The Chautauquan Daily columnist George Cooper wrote about an event titled *Some Banners, Mosaics, Postcards and Cartoons at Chautauqua*:

"The Chautauqua Oliver Archives Center can be a quiet place — all those dusty documents. But not today, when it hosts an absolute plethora of people and purposes: a banner tour with information on how those relics are restored and cared for . . . Charlotte Crittenden, banner committee member and year-round resident, will command the banner room in the Archives, answering questions about banners' upkeep and restoration. Of the 162 Chautauqua Literary and Scientific Circle banners, 54 have arrived in their resting place in the Archives. The others reside in Alumni Hall.

But images of all the banners are up to date and available in the banner book, *The Banners and Mosaics of Chautauqua* . . . originally compiled in 1992 by Ish Pedersen and recently updated by Mary Lee Talbot . . . in addition to the banners, the book includes images of the mosaics in the Hall of Philosophy, CLSC class symbols that speak to the educational concerns of each class."

CLSC BANNER – 1925 – The Kate Kimball Class

Photo by Selden Campen

Alumni Hall / Literary Arts Center – 1892/2009

Photo by Norman Karp

Members of the Chautauqua Literary and Scientific Circle (CLSC) classes of 1886-1895 built **Alumni Hall,** formerly the Union Class Building, in 1892. It was and is used for meetings and to display banners created by each year's class. The principal entry to the building is through a front parlor/office to a central hall, off of which there are a kitchen and four meeting rooms: the Dining Room, the Garden Room, the Library and the Kate Kimball Room (Kate Kimball was CLSC secretary from 1878, when she was 18, till her death in 1917). The library houses all of the CLSC book selections since its inception, while the other rooms and hallways display the historic CLSC Class Banners. Some particularly meaningful banners have been meticulously reproduced so that they may be displayed and enjoyed by all Chautauquans. The banners seldom leave Alumni Hall although approximately 40 are carried through parts of the grounds in the annual Recognition Day Parade.

Additional memorabilia are scattered throughout the building. Alumni Hall "oozes tradition and loveliness," said Bob Coghill, former archivist for the CLSC. The first floor of the building is principally used by the CLSC Alumni Association for organization and class meetings and classes on weekdays by Chabad Lubavitch of Chautauqua. The Chautauqua Writers' Center and the Chautauqua Special Studies Program share the second floor. The third floor space houses staff and faculty. Regular docent tours are available to the public for Alumni and Pioneer Halls.

Started by Bishop John Vincent and Lewis Miller, the CLSC is one of the oldest continuously-operating book club/home reading courses in America, as well

CLSC Fund Raising Event

Photo by Jeanne Wiebenga

as the oldest educational arm of Chautauqua Institution. While neither man had a college education, both felt that continuing education should be available for all. In 1878, more than 8,000 people signed up for the four-year guided reading program, and 1,708 actually graduated in 1882. Over the years, more than half a million readers have enrolled, and there existed as many as 10,000 reading circles worldwide where readers get together to discuss the books.

Building on the history of the CLSC, John and Georgia Court's and Mary Anne Morefield's gifts in 2009 provided for a much-needed renovation of Alumni Hall (a gift from the Alumni Association was later added) and helped to establish the literary arts as a major component of Chautauqua's program and elevated Chautauqua to be a nationally-recognized center for writers.

Oliver Archives Center – 1904 / 2004

The **Oliver Archives Center** houses Chautauqua Institution's collection of documents, photographs and artifacts related to its activities and affiliated organizations, such as the Chautauqua Women's Club and the Chautauqua Literary and Scientific Circle. Originally outside the gate, it was first a carriage house, then in succession a bindery, carpenter shop, piano tuning studio and opera rehearsal center. The 2004 renovation was made possible through the generosity of Hale and Judy Oliver.

Using a room-within-a-room approach creating a space between interior and exterior walls, condensation is prevented as the outside temperature changes. Temperature and relative humidity in the reading rooms and storage areas are separately controlled. Damage from ultra-violet light is lessened by coverings on windows and lights. Drainage systems, both within and outside the building, were improved during its renovation.

On the front entry level is a reading room designed to meet the needs of researchers. In the space below and attached to the original building is a textile storage area used for storage of CLSC banners.

In the reading room is the Seth Thomas clock used by the Institution for 80 years, first in the Old Pier Building and later in the Miller Bell Tower. Restoration was funded as a gift from Chloe and Bill Cornell.

Under the direction of Jon Schmitz, the Archives Department presents the Heritage Lecture Series biweekly throughout the season. Topics include early Chautauqua history, the "Chautauqua Movement," national trends that shaped or were shaped by Chautauqua and the extremely popular series known as "The Heroes of Chautauqua." Archivist Schmitz had the vision to start this program and, through his capable hands, has created one of the most popular afternoon activities on the grounds.

Prior Chautauqua archivists include Alfreda Irwin, to whom we are indebted for her efforts over many years in preserving Chautauqua stories, records and memorabilia. Her book *Three Taps of the Gavel* is most valuable in this regard.

Photo from the Chautauqua Archives

The Oliver Archives Center is staffed by a full time archivist assisted by a number of part-time positions, interns and volunteers. The public is welcome to visit the Archives during open hours and by appointment.

Note: The author of this book initiated, and together with family funded, "The Richard Newman Campen *Chautauqua Impressions* Fund." Originally intended to sponsor morning lectures, the fund most recently has supported the Chautauqua Archives Department programs.

Banner storage area is below the lawn and garden to the right of Oliver Archives Center.

Photo by Selden Campen

Everett Jewish Life Center – 2009

One of the newest of nearly 20 denominational houses, **The Everett Jewish Life Center** (EJLC), an Arts and Crafts shingle style building surrounded by beautiful gardens, is located at **36 Massey Avenue**. Designed by architect and life-long Chautauquan George W. Schnee, the three-story, 7,600 square foot building continues the Chautauqua tradition of large and inviting porches that foster community and welcome casual and spontaneous conversation.

The Everett Jewish Life Center, dedicated in July 2009, provides a focus for Jewish and interreligious events on the grounds. The Center was built with a generous gift from New York businesswomen, activist, and philanthropist Edith Everett and her family in honor and memory of her husband Henry Everett.

A place of welcome for the Jewish and larger Chautauqua community and visitors to gather, the building includes a large community room (serving both as a lounge and a lecture hall), a dining room, an unsupervised kosher kitchen, and a library and five rooms with private baths on the second floor that are used for guests and speakers.

Part of the original vision for the EJLC was that it be eco-friendly, incorporating the latest in building efficiencies and design. In its first year it received a Chautauqua Institution Green Merit Recognition Award.

The Everett Jewish Life Center fully participates in the Institution's nine themed weeks with a plethora of activities that inspire Jewish visitors and engage the broader community. Its Jewish film series, brown bag lunches, book reviews and an array of thought-provoking speakers are presented throughout the summer. Also, Yiddish language conversations are held weekly.

EJLC File Photo

Front Porch – 1,300 sq. ft. conversation area.

EJLC Community Room (set up as lecture hall).

Photo by Selden Campen

EJLC Community Room

EJLC File Photo

EJLC Library

EJLC File Photo

EJLC File Photo

Denominational Houses Along the Brick Walk

Lutheran House at 25 Peck Avenue– 1925

Photo from Google Images

Episcopal House at 24 Peck Avenue– 1900

Painting from Episcopal House – Artist Unknown

Disciples of Christ House at 32 Clark Avenue – 1904

Photo from Google Images

Baptist House at 35 Clark Avenue – 1895

Photo by Selden Campen

Catholic House at 20 Palestine Avenue– 2004
(formerly the Russell Schall Cottage – 1893)

Photo from Google Images

Presbyterian House at 9 Palestine Avenue– 1891

Photo from Google Images

Methodist House at 14 Pratt Avenue – 1888

Photo from Google Images

Smith Wilkes Hall – 1924

Photo from The Chautauquan Daily – Kreable Young Staff Photographer

Summer at Chautauqua is largely an outdoor experience with presentations under a roof for shade and rainy day protection. As with the Amphitheater and Hall of Philosophy, Smith Wilkes Hall continues this architectural feature. The hall is located downhill of the Brick Walk, between Janes and Foster, on a block which (on the 1885 map of the Institution) was known as "Wild Wood Park." Built in 1924, it was one of two buildings donated by Mrs. A.M. Smith Wilkes. In addition to being used as a lecture hall, it is the headquarters of the Bird, Tree and Garden Club (BTG). Its elevated stage faces a mini-arena area for dance or musical groups, and tiered seats. Room darkening perimeter shades for video presentations help make the hall extremely versatile. Behind the stage is the BTG Board meeting room and below are a kitchen and public rest rooms. The Newbury Terrace and McKnight Gardens on the downhill side of the building are memorials to

two prominent BTG members. In 1974 Eleanor McKnight Haupt gave an enlargement of this garden with additional landscaping in memory of her mother.

The Bird, Tree and Garden Club is one of the very active organizations on the Chautauqua grounds providing extensive programming. It also maintains many facilities for Chautauquans to learn and commune with nature; among them are its outdoor classrooms described elsewhere in this book, as well as the Arboretum on Wythe at the south end of the grounds, the Butterfly Garden near the entrance to the South Lot on Massey, the Louise Miller Igo Garden at the Main Gate and the Sensory Garden at the Children's School.

Smith Wilkes Hall interior.

Photo by Selden Campen

Gingerbread House – 1891

Photo by Selden Campen

The **Gingerbread House**, as it is known, at **34 Janes** was built in 1891 on a pre-existing tent platform as a guesthouse. The Carrier family occupied it for five generations. Subsequently, it was sold to Pauline Francher, Chautauqua's librarian and author of *Chautauqua: Its Architecture and Its People*. The house has two doors opening onto a porch, both upstairs and down, for easy access to the out-of-doors. They also provide indication of how narrow the rooms are. The Gingerbread House was originally painted grey with red trim and a shed built onto the back of the house was a summer kitchen.

The house resides on one of the smallest lots in Chautauqua, but its location on the corner across from Lincoln Park draws notice to it. Together with Thumbelina, the Gingerbread House is among the most photographed residences in the Institution.

Lincoln Park

This rounded, triangular-shaped block between Palestine, Janes and Warren Avenues was originally occupied by the Morey Hotel, which advertised in *The Chautauquan* of 1905, a "large cool dining room with seating capacity for 170." Now Lincoln Park serves as an open field for children and family play, picnics, and on the day of Old First Night the picnic for residents of Areas 5 & 6 of the Chautauqua Property Owners Association. The park is dedicated to the memory of Louisa Lincoln (1839-1918).

Lincoln Park picnic on day of Old First Night

Photo by Selden Campen

Morley Hotel (formerly occupying Lincoln Park.

Chautauqua Archive Postcard

Irwin Cottage – 1887

Located at **39 Palestine**, the **Irwin Cottage** was purchased and renovated in 2005 by the Kilpatrick family. The structure which is thought to have originally been T-shaped with a partial cellar has had many additions over the years. The off-center gabled roof indicates the left front was added, as were the kitchen, bedroom and laundry on the back. In 1955, Forrest and Alfreda Irwin purchased the house. Mrs. Irwin was a former editor of The Chautauquan Daily, Archivist of the Institution and author of the ever-popular *Three Taps of the Gavel.*

Photo by Robert Cahn

Spencer Hotel – 1878

One of several turn-of-the-century hotels located on the grounds, the **Spencer** at **25 Palestine Avenue** is notable for its four stories of porches that echo the cottage architecture of the time and represent a uniquely American innovation. Within elegant rooms, guests have a view overlooking the Amphitheater or Lincoln Park. Rooms are named for and decorated in period furnishings of English writers and poets such as Dickens, Austin, Byron and Keats. The hotel offers a serene spa, morning breakfast and has elevators (not often found in Chautauqua) to service the upper floors. At one time it had an annex across the street. Condominium apartments replaced the annex around 1980.

Photo by Selden Campen

The Cow House – 1875

For the past 30 years, Chautauqua families have known this quirky old cottage as **The Cow House** because of the cement cow that still grazes at **27 Waugh**. Farley & Ingrid Toothman, of Greene County, Pennsylvania, placed it there so their children would know where to come home. They bought the property in 1991, sold it in 2003 and bought it back in 2013.

A tent platform on this triangular lot was built and leased in 1875 to Abraham Bashline, a Methodist Episcopal minister. The lease was later assigned to the Prentiss Brown family who, in 1939, obtained outright ownership as the Institution maneuvered through the Great Depression. What started as being far away from the original speaker's grove, had become just steps away from the Amphitheater. The living room floor is still the original tent platform.

From 1954 to 1984 Miss Helen Lockwood owned 27 Waugh. She surely was a Chautauquan – teacher, principal and girl's basketball coach. She spent summers on the porch hosting tea parties. Miss Lockwood played bridge to win, was a member of the CLSC and Women's Club, and served as the long-time President of the International Order of King's Daughters and Sons.

Cow Adorning Cow House at 27 Waugh

Photo by Farley Toothman

Maple Inn – 1894

Photo by Jeanne Wiebenga

The **Maple Inn** is located at **8 Bowman** on the corner with Wythe. Susan Bauer told us it was built in 1894. However, the property was leased as early as 1879 to Wilson Jones of Greenfield, Pennsylvania on which they most likely had a tent platform dwelling.

In 1939 the property at the corner and next door were acquired by the Robinson family who combined the then existent structures into a single rooming house consisting of 27 rooms and 3 bathrooms (one on each floor). In 1968 Tom and Linda Krueger acquired the property and over time renovated it to be a year round inn with 12 apartments. Among other notables, Paul Newman and Joanne Woodward stayed at the Inn while their daughter Melissa studied dance.

Susan Bauer and her husband Todd founded and manage the Maple Group, a real estate brokerage firm, named after the Inn. Susan Krueger Bauer was raised in the Inn that she and her husband acquired from her parents. They are now raising their own family in the same structure, but in the grand fourth floor walk-up apartment they added in 2007 with a view overlooking Chautauqua Lake.

Carey Cottage Inn – 1896

The **Carey Cottage Inn** at **9 Bowman Avenue** is where George Gershwin stayed while he was composing his "Concerto in F." The rear apartment on the lower level was once the Rhapsody Café in honor of Mr. Gershwin.

The Carey is an example of the Second Empire style that was extremely popular at the turn of the nineteenth century. Built in 1896 the hotel consists of many units joined together. The three-story building with mansard roof has a clapboard exterior and is painted white on the first two levels and green on the third. There is a square green elevator shaft on the Wythe side of the building. At one time the Carey had forty employees.

An overpass was built when the Carey consisted of buildings on either side of Bowman. It was removed in 1991 when the building south of Bowman was sold to Mary and Gary Doebler, its current owners. Richard and Rita Paul retained the other building at 33 Miller, now known as Paul Manor.

Off the main entrance of the Carey is a reception hall and dining room to the right and a comfortable lounge on the left; however, when the weather is right, tenants prefer sitting and conversing on the front porch.

Photo by Selden Campen

The Paul Manor – Circa 1911

In the author's opinion, the most interesting, well-portioned portico in Chautauqua belongs to **The Paul Manor** located at **33 Miller Avenue**. It was once part of the Carey Hotel. The two buildings were connected by a third floor overpass that crossed Bowman, connecting the front of the Carey Hotel to the back of what is now known as Paul Manor. Richard and Rita Paul sold the Carey Hotel, removed the connecting overpass, and renamed this structure the Paul Manor. They converted it to an apartment cooperative. Smaller units sold for as little as $28,000 each in 1995.

Photo by Selden Campen

Miller Avenue

Robert Jeffrey's Painting of Miller Ave.
(from left to right - #30 The Holland House, #28 The Magee Manor & #26 The Fair Point Cottage)

Painting by Robert Jeffrey

Reformed Church House - 1883

Photo by Selden Campen

The Bee Haven – 36 Miller Avenue

Photo by Donna Brenner

The **Reformed Church House** at **10 Pratt Avenue** on the corner with Miller Avenue, built in 1883, is maintained by The Chautauqua United Church of Christ Society to provide affordable accommodations for members. You do not have to be a member of a UCC congregation to join the Chautauqua UCC Society. Annual or lifetime memberships is open to all individuals regardless of race, sex, national origin, religion, economic status, or sexual orientation. The UCC Society also manages the **Mayflower** at **4 Bowman Avenue** for the same purpose.

The Reformed Church House was owned by the Reformed Church of America before its merger with the Congregational Church in 1957.

Enjoying a tram ride on Miller Avenue are Steven Longstreth, Peter Campen and Sarah Campen Cheng

Photo by Selden Campen

Faithful Remnant – 1879

The **Faithful Remnant** at **27 Miller Avenue** is one of the most well preserved cottages within the institution. Robert Jeffrey acquired the cottage in 2011 and restored it shortly thereafter. He painted the watercolor of his house to the right. Mr. Jeffrey carried more than his share in bringing the 2014 revision of the Architecture and Land Use Regulations of the Institution to fruition. He was a major player on the Chautauqua Property Owners Association board and is currently a member of the Institution Board of Trustees.

J.O. Swan built the cottage on a pre-existent tent platform in 1879. Later, a kitchen was added on the right side of the house near the rear. The first floor living room is still lit by a natural gas lamp with pipes on the wall. Upstairs the linoleum coverings, from the 1930s with 70 years of built up paste wax, were restored and are now on display.

The Simpson family acquired the cottage in 1975. Clyde Simpson was manager of the Institution's Main Gate for many years and his son, Jeffrey Simpson, is the author of *A Chautauqua Utopia*. The Smucker family, of jam and jelly fame, purchased the cottage in 2002. Mr. R.K. Smucker was a speaker on the Amphitheater stage during Ethics Week in 2004.

Painting by Robert Jeffrey

Campen Inn – 1881

The **Campen Inn** at **34 Miller**, originally a rooming house known in the early 1900s as the Linwood Cottage, was built in 1881 with a front-facing gable built on a pre-existent tent platform. The Wingerd family acquired the house in 1923 and raised the left dormer in 1948, resulting in removal of the Victorian roofline. Alan Nelson purchased the house in 1965, raised the right dormer in 1971 and converted the ten upstairs rooms to three apartments. Alan's wife, Jane, is well known for her line drawings of Chautauqua buildings used for calendars, postcards, pamphlets and brochures.

Selden Campen, the author of this book, and his wife Jackie acquired the property in 1987, updated all interior spaces and added the third floor porch. At the Campen Inn we learned the true meaning of AT&T's ad, "Reach out and touch someone," easily done through our rear first floor windows.

Serendipity House

Photo by Ernie Mahaffey

Bob and Alma Sarver acquired the house at **40 Miller** in 1977 after having first purchased 38 Miller in 1972. Five years later, they purchased 26 Center. Bob had retired from a jewelry business in Saxonburg, Pennsylvania. He maintained his three homes meticulously and prided himself on his tool collection that he made available to the neighborhood. Alma used antiques, quilts and baskets profusely in decorating 40 Miller. Together they cared for Chautauqua's stray cat population as daily one or the other ventured with chow to wherever they had established their cat feeding station.

In 2012 Ernie Mahaffey, entrepreneur and former international distributor, and Sheila Penrose, corporate director and Chautauqua Institution Board of Trustees member, purchased the house, named it the **Serendipity House**, renovated the apartments, and expanded the deck and porch areas.

Photo by Selden Campen

Peony Cottage – 1879

Photo by Robert Cahn

One of the houses that catches the eye, on a picturesque street in Chautauqua, is **22 Center**, also known as the **Peony Cottage** (supposedly for the beautiful peonies that at one time must have been planted along the foundation). This Carpenter Gothic cottage was built in 1879 on an 1876 tent platform. Entirely original is the latticework in the gable peak, filling the triangular spaces formed by the vertical knop and collar. The dainty open arches make a "triptych" of the porch.

Louise Crouch, whose family built the Lutheran House, acquired the Peony Cottage in 1953. The cottage was purchased in 1969 and winterized by Fred and Helen Theuer. Mrs. Theuer was a long-time director of the CLSC and a devoted Chautauquan. Full-season Chautauquans Jim and Carol Chimento purchased the Peony Cottage in August, 2001 and remain the current owners. Jim Chimento serves on the board of the CLSC Science Group.

Christian Science Denominational House – 1881

Photo by Selden Campen

In 1949 the Chautauqua **Christian Science** Society purchased their **Denominational House** at **10 Center,** which had been the private residence of Edith Davenport of Rochester, New York for more than twenty years. The chapel next to the home was added circa 1960.

The reading room on the first floor of the house is open to the public and must be one of Chautauqua's least known benefits. The high quality Christian Science Monitor, now a weekly magazine rather than a daily newspaper, and a host of other materials are available there.

Logan Dormitory – 1890

Located at **17 Vincent** at the corner of Pratt and Vincent, **Logan Dormitory** has served many purposes. Originally, it was the private home of the Martin family of Pittsburgh. Mrs. Lewis Lapham of New York City funded its acquisition by the YWCA in 1918, which in 1922 opened the YWCA Hospitality House. In 1965 Mrs. Harry A. Logan funded its acquisition by the Institution to be used as a dormitory for summer school students. In 1991 the Logan Gallery was opened on the first floor as an exhibition space for the Chautauqua School of Art. In 2010 The Chautauquan Daily editorial and business offices relocated to what is now called Logan Hall. They were formerly in the Post Office Building and later in Kellogg Hall,

Logan Hall's distinguishing features are the Palladian window in the gable and the articulated round tower with conical cap to its side. It might be described as mildly eclectic Queen Anne style.

Photo from the Chautauquan – Ray Downey photographer

St. Elmo Hotel – 1890, Rebuilt 1988

In 1988 the **St. Elmo Condominiums** at **1 Pratt Avenue** were built on the site of the former St. Elmo Hotel, at the corner of Pratt and Ames on Bestor Plaza. Controversial as it was, the new owner's representatives, Richard and Joretta Speck, with claims backed by architects, successfully argued that the old hotel could not be saved, before the Institution issued a demolition permit. It is winterized for year-round occupancy, and has 61 residential apartments above several commercial units on the lower level. These commercial units are a spa, restaurant, deli, gift shop and women's clothing stores.

Photo by Selden Campen

The original St. Elmo Hotel was an amalgam of buildings dating back to 1890. During the summer season it was alive with people. Off-season it catered to those who liked to be close to nature, read, ski, play bridge, do puzzles or just enjoy a quiet Chautauqua day. Its spacious lobby was a pleasant place to relax and its dining room a popular choice in season. Today, Chautauquans still remember its grand reception desk and the harp in the lobby, which was regularly played in concert. The movie "St. Elmo's Fire" was inspired by a bellhop's experiences working at the old hotel.

Chautauqua Archive Postcard

Bailey's Interiors – Circa 1895

**St. Elmo Hotel at left; Colonnade at right
Bailey's Interiors in the middle.**

Painting by Jerome Chesley

Diane and Jack Bailey have been selling furniture, antiques and accessories at **Bailey's Interiors**, on the corner of Ames and Pratt, since they acquired it in 1989. At the time of this writing the property is for sale, so its future as a retail outlet is unclear.

The first lessee of **2 Ames** was Hiram A. Pratt, who had been put in charge of the grounds by the Erie Conference of the Methodist Episcopal Church and later its successor, the Chautauqua Lake Sunday School Assembly. These were the sponsoring organizations of the Chautauqua Lake Camp Meeting Association. Mr. Pratt was commended for the skillful way he marked and felled the trees as he cleared the land for meeting sites and cottages. Pratt Avenue, one of Chautauqua's principal streets, is named for him.

Photo by Selden Campen

Tally-Ho – 1881

At **16 Morris** is the **Tally-Ho**, a Victorian hotel furnished with antiques. Formerly the Ohio Cottages, it was acquired and renamed by the Streeter family in 1942. The Tally-Ho is centrally located on the grounds just off Bestor Plaza. The restaurant provides both full service and cafeteria style dining three meals a day.

Photo by Selden Campen

Unitarian-Universalist Denominational House – 1878/2009

The **Unitarian Universalist Fellowship of Chautauqua**, formed in 1979, conducts Sunday services in the Hall of Philosophy. In 2008 they purchased the house at **6 Bliss** to serve as a gathering place and to offer affordable housing on the Institution grounds.

UU Denominational House at 6 Bliss

Photo from www.uufchautauqua.org

After interior renovations by the UUFC, the structure has 7 bedrooms, 4 baths, living room, dining room, kitchen and a large partially shaded rear patio. In addition to denominational activities, meeting weekly at the UU House are the Chautauqua Dialogues (sponsored by Chautauqua Department of Religion) and PFLAG (Parents and Friends of Lesbians and Gays). The left

Rear Patio at 6 Bliss

Photo by Selden Campen

Painting by Carol Hopper

section of 6 Bliss dates from circa 1878. The Levinson family purchased the house in 1969 from the owners of the TallyHo, renovated it and added a one-story extension – now the middle section of the building. In the 1990s, the Levinsons added the two-story addition on the right.

Previously from 1904 to 1963, the national **Unitarian Universalist Association** had maintained a denominational house at **26 Cookman Avenue** adjacent to the Hall of Philosophy. It was sold due to the national organization's financial distress.

1904-1963 UU House adjacent to Hall of Philosophy

Queen Anne style for its prerequisite bay windows, multiple roofs meeting at right angles, polygonal turret, and large porch gable.

Chautauqua Archives Photo

Thumbelina – 1873

Photo by Richard Campen

At **10 Morris Avenue** tucked between the Colonnade and the post office is **Thumbelina**. Built on a tent platform in 1873, it is of classic Victorian design, ornamented with mortised knop and collar members, wood-laced bracketing on the porch supports and is decorated with carpenter gothic gingerbread railings. This private residence is one of the most photographed homes within the Institution.

Water Filtration Plant and Publications Office

On Ramble behind the Colonnade is a building dating back to the 1920s. It is shared by the Chautauqua Publications Office and the Chautauqua Utility District Water Filtration Plant. The **Water Filtration Plant** at **1 Ramble** supplies the Institution with 600,000 gallons of purified water per day from Chautauqua Lake. The Chautauqua **Publications Office** is open to all Chautauquans for duplication services and office supply purchases.

Until recently, the Chautauqua Women's Club held their annual Flea Market in the rear of the Colonnade Building. This had been one of the popular events of the season. One man's junk turns into another's treasure. The annual Flea Market has been replaced with Flea Boutiques throughout the season.

Photo by Selden Campen

Photo by Selden Campen

Fowler-Kellogg Art Center – 1889/2010

Photo by Robert Cahn

The **Fowler-Kellogg Art Center** opened in 2010. A major gift of Charlotte and Chuck Fowler and leadership gifts by the Gallo Family, Gloria Plevin, Kathy Hancock, and Lauren Fine enabled the transformation of the then 121 year-old iconic building into art galleries. Visual Arts at Chautauqua (VACI) now has 3,600 square feet of gallery for its several exhibitions per season. Among them is The Chautauqua School of Art Annual Student Exhibition, wherein students may sell their art.

The front of Fowler-Kellogg Art Center is a shining example of the Queen Anne Style, while on the rear of the building a contemporary veranda was added, complete with small cafe for lunch or afternoon snacks. The art center interior has soft lighting, coffered wooden ceilings and Brazilian cherry hardwood floors.

In 1889 James M. Kellogg built Anne M. Kellogg Hall in memory of his mother and gifted it to the Chautauqua Sunday School Assembly. Kellogg Hall was located on what is now Bestor Plaza, directly across Pratt from the St. Elmo Hotel. In 1905, it was moved to its present location in order to provide more open playground space. Kellogg Hall has served as the Women's Christian Temperance Union (WCTU) headquarters, the Chautauqua Special Studies Program registrar's office, and the business and editorial offices of The Chautauquan Daily before becoming the art gallery it is today.

Behind Fowler-Kellogg is the Strohl Art Center, also renovated in 2010. Together Fowler-Kellogg and **Strohl Art Center**s have substantially increased Chautauqua's gallery space.

Fowler-Kellogg Art Center veranda.

Strohl Art Center

Trina Turturici preparing her exhibition entry.

Chautauqua file photo

Chautauqua file photo

Photo from The Chautauquan Daily - Benjamin Host Staff Photographer

Hurlbut Memorial Church – 1931

Photo by Jeanne Wiebenga

Hurlbut Memorial Church, named for one of the most beloved Chautauqua figures, Dr. Jesse Hurlbut, was built in 1931. Author and educator, Hurlbut was involved in religious studies. He died in 1930, six years after celebrating 50 summers at Chautauqua. Beginning in 1875, Hurlbut taught adult Bible classes and assisted the CLSC, and also supervised Chautauqua's Normal Courses. He succeeded Dr. John Vincent as editor of the Methodist Episcopal Sunday School publications. His *Story of Chautauqua* is one of the most definitive histories of the Institution and he is also well known as author of a book for children, *Story of the Bible.*

Otis Johnson designed Hurlbut Church. First plans for the Church located it on Pratt Avenue facing Bestor Plaza. The building features art deco stained glass windows and an organ donated by the Welch (grape juice) family of Westfield, New York. Hurlbut serves as a community church for residents both on and off the grounds during the off-season. Prior meeting places had been the Old Chapel (where Smith Memorial Library now stands), Higgins Hall, and the Methodist Denominational House.

Hurlbut Church now functions under the direction of the United Methodist Church. In the summer, lunch is served weekdays and dinner on Thursday evenings for nominal prices. The large meeting room in the basement is made available to many organizations, including the Chautauqua Property Owners Association for its annual June pot luck dinner just before the start of the season and the Hebrew Congregation for both their Saturday morning services and Sunday evening lectures series.

Hurlbut's main entrance under the balcony.

Photo by Selden Campen

Hurlbut's nave.

Photo by Selden Campen

These two interior photos to of Hurlbut Memorial Church were taken as the Hebrew Congregation was entering the sanctuary for a Sunday evening lecture. Note the lovely stained glass windows, coffered ceiling and Romanesque arches.

Bratton Theater – 1885/2000

Painting by Robin K. Robins

The **Bratton Theater**, built in 1885, is one of the oldest public buildings on the grounds. In this building, originally Normal Hall, were taught "Normal" courses for Sunday School teachers, which was Chautauqua's reason-to-be at that time. Circa 1950, a second interior storey was removed, leaving one great hall with a high cathedral ceiling supported by four massive laminated wooden arches. The horizontal iron tie rods were added a few years after the roof was built to keep the wood arches from flexing outward due to Chautauqua's exceptionally heavy snow loads. Modern computer structural analysis confirmed that the original carpenters were skillful enough to locate the tie rods within inches of the ideal location. The porch appended to the hall bears an interesting, sawn-art, geometric design in its gable.

Many theater companies have performed at Chautauqua over the last century, including the Cleveland Playhouse, which made Chautauqua Institution its summer home for 51 years, beginning in 1930. During that time, Normal Hall also served as the rehearsal hall and scene shop for the Chautauqua Opera Company. In the early 1980s the prestigious Acting Company made Chautauqua a recurring stop on their national touring circuit. This brought Michael Kahn to the grounds of Chautauqua, and under his leadership, the Chautauqua Conservatory Theater Company was created in 1983 and Normal Hall became a dedicated theater space.

Normal Hall was transformed into the beautiful, 269-seat Bratton Theater (named for the Institution's 15th president, Daniel Bratton), a major accomplishment in both preservation and renovation, under the direction of architect Mitchell Kurtz, in 2000. The renovation garnered several awards.

Photo by Selden Campen

Photo from www.robertdavis.com

Norton Hall – 1929

Norton Memorial Hall – 1929

Built in 1929, **Norton Memorial Hall** was a gift from Lucy Coit Fanning Norton in memory of her husband Oliver Wilcox Norton of Civil War fame, and her daughter Ruth. The project was managed by her son Ralph Norton, who later became Chautauqua's 7th president. The architect was Otis Johnson of Chicago. The hall seats an audience of 1,356. It is the home of the Chautauqua Opera Company, and for 50 years had been the summer home of the Cleveland Playhouse. By terms of the gift, operas performed in the hall must be performed in English.

Farewell banquet on the Norton Hall stage for Jay Lessinger - 21 years Chautauqua Opera Co, manager.

Photo by Selden Campen

Norton Memorial Hall is Art Deco in style and constructed of concrete. Cast against wooden forms, the timber lines of which can be seen at close range, the Hall is considered to be one of the first poured in situ, monolithic buildings in the eastern United States.

The building is distinguished in that it incorporates more art in its design than any other structure in Chautauqua. It is decorated with panels designed by sculptors Fred and Mabel Torrey; their fountain sculpture, now in front of the post office building, was originally designed for and placed in front of Norton Hall. The large rectangular relief sculpture at the upper left corner of the facade, with a nude at its center, de-

Norton Hall lobby following its 2015 facelift.

Photo from The Chautauquan Daily – Ruby Wallau Staff Photographer

picts "The Birth of Beauty" and that in the upper right corner is entitled "Moods of Music." Inside, across the proscenium arch, is the inscription "All passes, art alone endures," which is attributed to French poet, dramatist, novelist, journalist, and art and literary critic Theophile Gautier.

Despite interior painting and upgrades, Norton Hall remains in need of repair; during a summer performance it cries out for air conditioning. Richard Campen, in his 1984 book, *Chautauqua Impressions,* wrote "Virtually untouched since its construction 54 years ago, there are extensive plans afoot to restore and modernize the building."

Ticket gazebo before Norton Hall

Photo by Selden Campen

Pre-performance serenade by music school students.

Photo by Selden Campen

Florence Hall – 1892

The International Order of the King's Daughters and Sons (IOKDS) has been on the grounds since 1920. Its first dorm was the Benedict House at 34 Vincent, acquired in 1928. In 1944, the IOKDS recognized the need for a second residence to house a growing number of students in its scholarship program, for which Florence Roblee, an IOKDS member, offered **6 Irving Place**, built in 1892. Upon acceptance, the house was named in her honor. In its early days, the scholarship program was for young women only. After 1953 when it was opened to young men, **Florence Hall** was referred to as the women's residence and Bonnie Hall, at 29 Vincent was purchased for the use of men.

Photo by Selden Campen

Pickens House – 1877

Irving Place was in the northwest corner of the 50-acre parcel purchased in 1874 at Fair Point for the first Chautauqua Sunday School Assembly. The tax assessor's records show there has been a cottage on **2 Irving Place** since 1877. Richard and Betty Pickens purchased the property in 1955. Co-owners Francie Pickens Oliver and nephew Mike Springer have maintained this modest home to the extent possible in its original state, including the kitchen. Note the great view of the lake, the dock, the lower lawn for field sports, and a sign; "Don't Mess with Texas," which indicates the long distance this family travels to be Chautauquans.

The Gleason – 1887

The property at **32 North Lake Drive** gets its name from the 1873 Chautauqua Lake Camp Meeting Association lease to William S. Gleason. In 1933 the Gleason family defaulted on a loan from the State Bank of Mayville, which held the property, and it was transferred to the Giffords in 1939. Paul and Pat King purchased **The Gleason** in 1969 and Pat still manages it today. It is the only remaining rooming house that is located directly on the lake. The Gleason is "Old Chautauqua" and is beautifully maintained.

Photo by Selden Campen

One Root – President's House

Photo by Selden Campen

One Root, built in the Queen Anne style in 1896, was the home of several Chautauqua presidents, from Bestor to Remick. Franklin and Eleanor Roosevelt, Amelia Earhart, and Admiral Richard Byrd were among the many notables entertained at The President's House. The garden facing North Lake Drive was the scene of many gala receptions, and it was here that John Phillip Sousa gave a band concert. The home was remodeled and winterized in 1962 for President Curtis Haug.

In 1972, under Oscar Remick's presidency, 1501 North Lake Drive became the president's home. Then Chairman of the Board Richard Miller, grandson of Founder Lewis Miller, and his family purchased the house from the Institution and became occupants of One Root.

Studebaker House – 1902

The **Studebaker House** built in 1902 at **39 North Lake Drive** is important both for its distinctive architecture and the people who lived there. Clement Studebaker, automobile mogul and second President of Chautauqua, purchased the property from Dr. Jesse Hurlbut who had built a house there in 1887. The Hurlbut house was moved a block away and became the basis for what is now the Gleason Hotel.

C.T. Terrill, Nina Terrill Wensley's father, purchased the 39 North Lake Drive cottage in 1916, later selling it to the Peters family of Oil City, Pennsylvania in 1933. Albertus Rappole became the owner in 1962, and Francesca Rappole, Chautauqua trustee and president of the Bird, Tree and Garden Club, later became the owner.

The house is in the Dutch architectural style. Its gambrel roof extends over the front porch, which offers a fine view of the lake. The construction is of grey clapboard; aluminum siding was added later. Mrs. Rappole added a large library and entertained many prominent officials in her home, including former president Gerald Ford, a close friend of her brother, Senator Charles Goodell.

Photo by Selden Campen

Photo by Selden Campen

Steamboat House – 1890

Theodore Flood, editor of The Chautauquan Daily, built this architectural jewel, the **Steamboat House**, at **45 North Lake Drive** in 1890. Dr. Flood was a printer from Meadville, Pennsylvania. The porch, which runs the full length of the front and around the side, was partially enclosed in 1892. Wood siding was put on the house between 1969 and 1971. There are cupolas or turrets above the porch at each end of the house.

Caroline King, wife of Jules King and grandmother of Mrs. Frank Karslake, purchased the Steamboat House in 1900. The Kings traveled extensively and filled the house with ceramic and brass pieces. The house passed to her daughter and grandson who owned it until 1958, when George and Helen Cornell purchased it. George was a member of the Chautauqua Board of Trustees and Helen was president of the Friends of the Library.

President William McKinley was a houseguest while governor of Ohio.

Farrar House – 1890

Charles Farrar of Akron, Ohio built **43 North Lake Drive** on the corner at Hurst Avenue in 1890. The **Farrar House** was the first home on the Chautauqua grounds to be electrified, though they had to wait three years for the lights to be turned on since there was no generator at Chautauqua. Charles Case, grandson of Farrar, worked for Thomas Edison at his factory in Orange Park, New Jersey.

The structure is a typical Victorian style house with a first floor porch having a fine view of the lake. A railing with wide posts supports the porch roof, which has a cupola in the center. It is covered with green clapboard.

John H. Rogers, current owner and summer resident, is a relative of Francis Willard, president of the WCTU in 1879 and instrumental in the passage of Women's Suffrage and Prohibition amendments to the US Constitution.

Photo by Selden Campen

Iconic View of The Miller Bell Tower From North Lake Drive

55 North Lake Drive – 1985 President's House

The current **President's House** at **55 North Lake Drive** is Victorian in style and looks as though it had stood there for many decades. When the Institution decided to build a new residence for Dan Bratton, the 15th President of Chautauqua, it selected 100 feet along North Lake Drive, comprised of 40 feet of Harris Avenue (never developed) and 60 feet carved out of College Hill Park. The lot extends up the hill 110 feet. Frequent dinners for notable speakers, performers dig-

Photo by Selden Campen

Corner Gazebo at the 55 N Lake Dr. President's House

Photo from The Chautauquan Daily – Ellie Haugsby Staff Photographer

nitaries, other guests of the Institution and large fund raisers are conducted in or beside the house, depending on the number invited. Pictured behind the house and its northwest corner gazebo is a gathering of the NOW Generation, a group of philanthropic supporters at Chautauqua under the age of 50.

University Beach

Chautauqua maintains four public beaches and stations lifeguards at them during regularly established hours. They include University Beach at the foot of College Hill, Pier Beach next to the Pier Building, Children's Beach adjacent to Pier Beach, and Heinz Beach at the northerly entrance to the youth activity area.

University Beach and College Hill are named for Chautauqua's College of Liberal Arts, located at the top of the Hill until 1918. The College granted degrees from 1883 to 1892.

Photo by Selden Campen

College Hill Park

Photo by Selden Campen

In 1880 Mr. James M. Hunt sold 50.4 acres to the Chautauqua Lake Sunday School Assembly, and together with an additional tenth of an acre parcel purchased at the same time, extended the Assembly's northerly boundary from approximately what is now Scott Avenue to about Prospect Avenue. The purchases brought the total area of the Grounds up to about 139 acres.

Much of the new land was set apart for public parks and Summer School purposes. Harris Avenue was intended to reach from Pratt Avenue to North Lake Drive, but its lower end was never developed, along with several other streets that would have cut through the park.

Strohl House – 1940

Photo by Selden Campen

In 1972 the house at **68 North Lake Drive** became the home for Chautauqua's presidents. Many of the artists and government officials presented on the Chautauqua platform have been entertained here. They include Theodore Morrison, George Shearing, Peter Nero, Roger Williams, Gov. Malcolm Wilson, and Lt. Gov. Mary Krupsak of New York.

Walter Shaw, Vice President of G.C. Murphy Company and Chairman of the Chautauqua Board of Trustees, built the house in 1940. He and his family lived here until Chautauqua Institution purchased it with the help of the Gebbie Foundation. Oscar Remick and his family were the first presidential family of Chautauqua to occupy this home.

The house commands a fine view of Chautauqua Lake. Among the impressive receptions held here was the one to celebrate the Chautauqua Commemorative Stamp issued during the Chautauqua Centennial.

After the succeeding President's House was built at 55 North Lake Drive for the Bratton family, Dr. Lowell Strohl and his wife Rebecca purchased this house in 1984. The Strohl family still resides in the house. They have been major donors to the Institution, including the Strohl Art Center on Wythe at Ramble Avenue behind the Fowler- Kellogg Art Center.

Hagan Residence – 1992

Photo by Selden Campen

Thomas and Susan Hagan built their Chautauqua home in 1992 at **4 Prospect**, overlooking University Beach and College Park. It is a contemporary one and one-half story house with a large dormer, open on three sides, rising from the gabled roof oriented parallel to Prospect Avenue. The expansive ground-level front porch continues a Chautauqua tradition, enabling conversation with those who pass by. A modest ranch style home, built in 1964, previously occupied the property.

Susan Hagan died in 2015; the family continues to reside here. A fourth generation and lifelong Chautauquan, she served on the Board of Trustees from 1991 to 1999. In 1986, Mr. and Mrs. Hagan were delegates to the first Conference on U.S./Soviet Relations, sponsored by the Institution and the Eisenhower World Affairs Institute, held in Riga, Latvia.

Most enduring of her gifts of talent and funds to Chautauqua is the renovation of the Wensley Guest House, now named the Hagan-Wensley Guest House in her honor. Amphitheater lecturers and performers are provided a room at the Hagan-Wensley Guest House.

Logan House – 1959

The property at **8 Prospect** was first deeded to Evangeline McKnight in 1952 and acquired by the Logan family in 1959. They built the **Logan House** that stands here today. Maritza Morgan, beloved Chautauqua artist and writer, painted the mural on this house to honor her husband, who was a member of the Chautauqua Symphony. Every painted face represents a member of the Symphony at the time.

Note the teacup sculpture on the side of the house. The teacup is in memory of "Chautauqua Tea" served on the front porches of this dry community, where written into property deeds were strict forfeiture clauses for violation of the temperance rules.

Photos by Selden Campen

Kanfer House – 2014

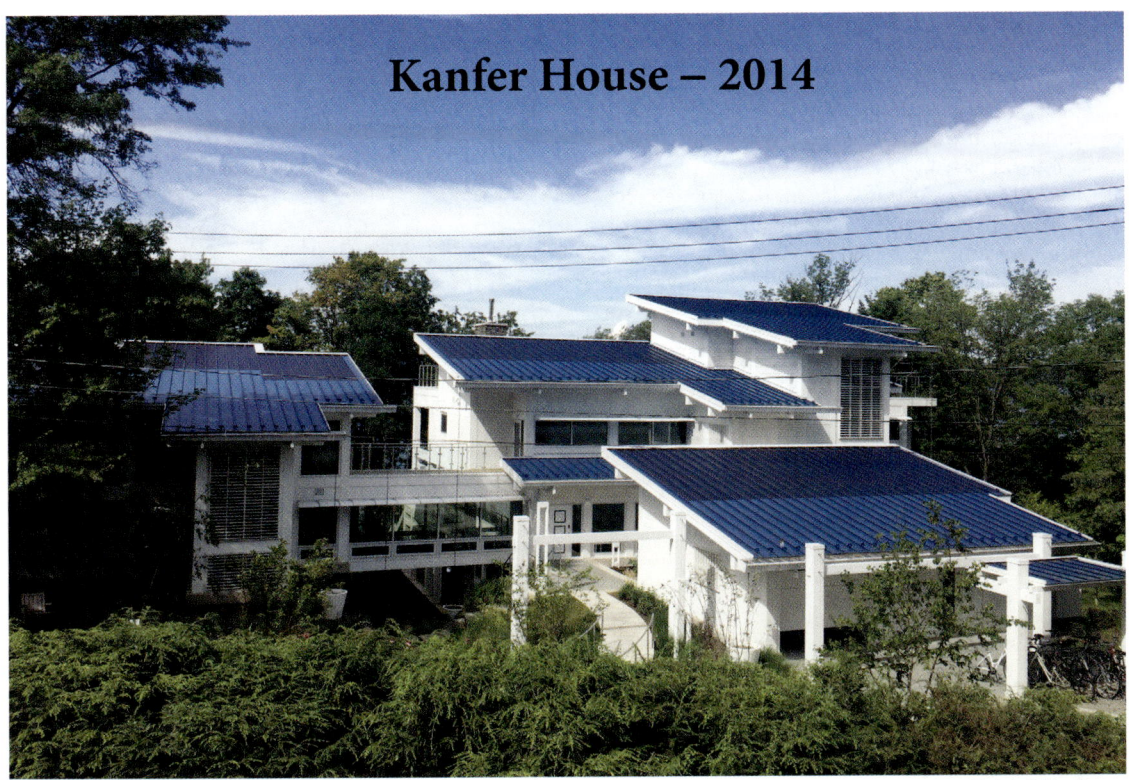

Photo by Selden Campen

Joe Kanfer built his house to accommodate the families of his four adult children, aunts, uncles, nieces, nephews, cousins, and a dozen grandchildren – a total of more than 40 people. From planning to completion, the house at **88 North Lake Drive** took five years. To view the structure at its best, one must ascend the hill opposite the house for an elevated unobstructed vantage point.

Marty Serena, known for his work in designing environmentally efficient buildings, was chosen as the architect for the **Kanfer House**. The Institution also selected Marty Serena's firm for its upcoming Amphitheater project. The Kanfer House excels in five factors due to extensive collaboration between family members and Mr. Serena. These include: 1) solar panels on a south facing roof to generate energy, 2) oversized gutters, augmented with descending chains to guide rainwater to cisterns for use within the house and to underground garden pipes, 3) installation of quality windows, 4) cre-

ating a well-sealed, air-tight building, and 5) orientation of the dwelling to include large south facing windows for absorption of radiant heat.

Joe and Pam Kanfer, of GOJO Industries, the manufacturer of Purell Hand Sanitizer, have been coming to Chautauqua since about 2005. They chose to build a home here for the benefit of their children. Mr. Kanfer said "It's not all about the opportunities with classes, Boys' and Girls' Club, and all the things they can do. The kids they're meeting here are also terrific kids that tend to be interested in learning. If you believe in learning, what a great place to be."

The previous owner of 88 North Lake Drive, Carol McCarthy Duhme, acquired this property in 1970. Circa 1975, the Duhmes moved the house from the corner of Oak Avenue and North Lake Drive across the street to this lake front lot. Removing that house, the Kanfers started with a blank slate and built a unique house that will grace Chautauqua for many generations.

Brigadoon – 2005

Photo by Selden Campen

Photos by Carolyn Lingenfelter

One of the more attractive homes along the water is the Jahrling House at **92 North Lake Drive**, known as **Brigadoon**. Looking down from the street above, an inviting swimming pool fronts a large three-story colonial home, with large porches in the rear facing Chautauqua Lake. On the northeast corner of the house is a multi-level octagonal turret enclosed on the second floor and open on the third. Robert and Gretchen Jahrling acquired the property in 1991.

The Jahrlings met at Chautauqua as teenagers in the 1940s when Robert was a lifeguard at the bathing beach and Gretchen worked at the Carey Hotel. They have spent almost every summer here since. They also own a house at 6 Peck Avenue, their first Chautauqua house, which they allow their children and grandchildren to use. Bob Jahrling and his family have been long-time members of the Chautauqua Yacht Club (CYC) and have competed quite successfully in the CYC sponsored C-Scow races.

Photo by Caroline Jahrling

Packard Manor -1915

Photo by Selden Campen

Born in Warren, Ohio, William Doud Packard was a manufacturer who in 1890, with his brother James, founded Packard Electric Company in Warren, Ohio and manufactured incandescent carbon arc lamps. The brothers, together with investor George L. Weiss, formed a partnership called Packard & Weiss that released its first automobile in 1899. The partnership became the Packard Motor Car Company, relocated to Detroit in 1903, and eventually merged with the Studebaker Corporation in 1954. The last Packard automobile was made in 1958.

Following Packard Motor Company's relocation

Packard Manor Tablet

The tablet in front of the Packard Manor reads, "The Packard Manor was built in 1915 as a private residence by William Doud Packard. It was completely renovated in 1999 by Mr. and Mrs. Reginald Lenna. Great care was given to restore the manor to its original style and grandeur. The manor still serves as a private residence.; Mr. and Mrs. Robert Metzger purchased the manor in 2009."

Photo by Selden Campen

to Detroit, the Packard brothers focused on making automotive electrical systems through the separate Packard Electric Company. GM acquired Packard Electric in 1932, renaming it Delphi Packard Electric Systems in 1995. The company was spun off and became independent of GM in 1999, and remains in business today.

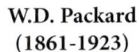
W.D. Packard (1861-1923)

Photo from Wikipedia

William and James Packard's father, Warren Packard, was a "pioneer" Chautauquan. William purchased 6.5 acres of land adjacent to the Chautauqua Institution overlooking the lake, and in 1915 he commissioned a summer home to be designed by a famous architectural firm in New York City, Warren and Wetmore, who were also the designers of the Grand Central Terminal in New York City. Inspired by Sir Winston Churchill's country house "Chartwell" in Kent, the house was the culmination of a dream long held by William Packard,

While overseas, William Packard suffered an insect bite that caused total blindness and confinement to a wheelchair. He was able to assist Warren & Wetmore in the design of his house by arranging models of component parts on a lapboard. The house was designed to be completely fireproof. Its walls are solid concrete poured over 8" steel girders. Its floors are one and one-

Packard Manor (Continued)

Photo by Josette Rolley

Photo by Matt Kleck — www.mkleckphotography.com

half feet thick concrete poured over 18" steel girders and covered with inlaid tiles. The brick veneer on the outside of the house was imported from England. The slate roof is comprised of shingles imported from Belgium, each weighing 36 pounds.

The Packard Manor has an elevator serving all four floors and an 80-foot long porch on the lakefront side. It had its own organ, which was eventually moved to the Hall of Christ, and later disposed of in 2000 when the Institution acquired the Tallman Tracker Organ. The first floor has a vestibule and a large central hall, flanked on the right by a large living room, and behind and to the left by a large dining room. Beyond the living room is a bricked study, formerly a solarium. Upstairs the Manor has twelve bedrooms and eight baths.

The **Packard Manor** at **10 Elm Street** was not completed until 1917. William Packard only lived in the house three years. Upon the owner's death the Manor fell into various hands and prior to 1942 it was used as a home for retarded children. It was in a state of disrepair when it was purchased by Mr. & Mrs. W.D. McCreary, who restored it to a private residence.

In 1957, Dr. & Mrs. Carl Winter, former moral and spiritual advisor as well as lecturer at General Motors Corporation, acquired the residence. The Winters entertained many famous people at Packard Manor, as did the Institution during the Chautauqua presidency of Curtis Haug (1964-1970). One such noteworthy event was the reception held for Indian Ambassador B.K. Ne-

hru, who left a signed copy of *Paintings of Sultans and Emperors of India* as a gift.

The Packard Manor still serves as a single-family residence, most recently in 1998 by Reginald and Elizabeth Lenna, who again restored the house and added a wing to the north, and then in 2009 by Robert and Sally Metzger.

A duplicate but smaller house with slightly revised plans was built in Warren, Ohio by Mr. Sanford White.

This book's author has intentionally excluded winter scenes since this is not the way most visitors experience Chautauqua. But this photo of a horse-driven sleigh passing the Packard Manor was too good to leave out.

Packard Manor

Photo from the Chautauqua Archive — Rosemary Rappole photographer — 2010

Chautauqua Lake

For those reading this book while walking the grounds, before turning up the hill at the north boundary of the Institution, recall the beautiful homes, lush green yards, parks, and a gorgeous lake that provides swimming, sailing, water skiing, and other leisure time activities for Chautauquans; but it was not always that way.

Things turned ugly on July 24, 2010. The author was on a sailboat earlier that day, the sky turned grey, it began to rain, and boaters headed for shore. An EF2 tornado (wind speeds between 111 and 135 mph) touched down in Mayville, damaged the Chautauqua Liquor and Wine store beyond repair, traversed the lake as a waterspout, and did more damage on the other side. It took more than a minute before the condensation funnel formed as the waterspout passed over the lake. At Chautauqua Lake Estates, the cyclone picked up a beached canoe of one unfortunate resident, and hurled it up the hillside through its owner's condo window.

The photo below was obtained from the Internet shortly after the event – photographer unknown.

Waterspout on Chautauqua Lake
July 24, 2010

NorthShore Townhomes – 1983

Built in 1983, **NorthShore Townhomes** at **20 Elm Street** consist of twelve Resorts Condominiums International (RCI) timeshares and 18 wholly owned units. Chautauqua Enterprises, Inc. advertised, "You don't have to give up the culture of Chautauqua to enjoy luxury living. You can have both with an exquisite NorthShore vacation home. Two bedrooms, fireplace, whirlpool bath, full kitchen, swimming pool and beautiful Chautauqua surroundings. You could make this kind of elegance part of your stay at Chautauqua through interval ownership. It's a practical plan allowing you to own a luxurious vacation home for as many weeks as you chose. For that time frame each year, it is yours to enjoy forever."

Residence Halls

Bellinger Hall – 1974

Chautauqua file photo

son, it houses art, music, dance and theater school students. Chautauqua On a Budget uses the Hall during the last two weeks of the season and Road Scholars use the Hall for weeklong programs before and after.

Dorm rooms are mainly doubles, but there are some triples and quads. Each room comes with a bed, desk and closet for each resident and a bathroom is shared with one other room.

Students who live in Chautauqua's residence halls are required to enroll in the full meal plan that includes breakfast, lunch and dinner seven days a week.

Photo by Selden Campen

At the intersection of Hedding and Evergreen Avenues stands Bellinger Hall, built as a year-round dormitory residence. Its name honors the generosity of former Chautauqua Institution Trustee Geraldine Gebbie Bellinger. Designed by architect Scott Lawson, the initial portion of Bellinger Hall was built in 1974 during the centennial year of the Institution. The idea of Functionalism carried out in this building follows the example of Frank Lloyd Wright. Subsequent additions have expanded its size to now accommodate 250 residents.

During the first seven weeks of Chautauqua's sea-

Connolly Residence Hall – 1924/2009

Connolly Residence Hall is a century-old facility renovated in 2009. It was a gift Jack and Marcia Connolly dedicated to The Chautauqua Opera Company. The building, formerly known as the Boys' Dormitory, was stripped to its studs and rebuilt to provide 30 modern rooms with privacy suitable for older students and staff. Unfortunately, Marcia Connolly did not live to see the dedication of the facility on July 18, 2009.

Photo by Selden Campen

Lincoln Dormitory – 1966

Photo by Selden Campen

Lincoln Dormitory is currently used as a girls-only facility. The dorm follows the external features of the neighboring Summer School buildings. Mrs. John C. Lincoln gave it as a centennial gift in 1966 in memory of her husband, an enthusiastic Chautauqua student even into his nineties.

Carnahan-Jackson Dance Studio – 1912/2008

Photo by Selden Campen

guess that some of the dancers are only 11 years old. In a July 11, 2015, story on dance in The Chautauquan Daily, dance faculty member Sarkis Kaltakchian said, "It is my goal to teach them as many different styles and different ways of moving as possible. The more ways their bodies move, the more versatile they become as dancers." He continues with a statement which could easily have been said by instructors in any of the professional level art schools conducted at Chautauqua, "I want them to work very hard, but at the same time I want them to love the art form. I want them to understand that hard work is a part of the passion. It's part of the reward at the end of the day when you perform well and feel you have improved."

Formerly known as the Lodge and used as an infirmary, the Carnahan-Jackson Dance Studio was renovated in 2008 as a gift of the Carnahan-Jackson Foundation. Dr. William S. Bainbridge of New York City, who brought his surgical patients to Chautauqua for recuperation, built it in 1912. The Dance Studio now houses the Chautauqua School of Dance and the Charlotte Ballet. It consists of four large teaching and rehearsal studios.

Upon peering into the Carnahan-Jackson Dance Studio during a dance rehearsal, it would be difficult to

Photo from The Chautauquan Daily – Bria Granville Staff Photographer

Arts and Crafts Quadrangle – 1909/1983/2009

The Arts and Crafts Quadrangle, also known as The Art Center, enjoys a beautiful vista of Chautauqua Lake from its perch on College Hill – the highest point on the grounds. The Quadrangle was built in three phases beginning in 1908 and ending in 1916. Phase I was ready for use in 1909. It was designed by Green and Wicks staff architect Franklyn Kidd, collaborating with Chautauqua's Summer Art Program Director Henry Turner Bailey. Later Mr. Bailey became head of The Cleveland School of Art in the early 1920s. The Bailey family has figured prominently in Chautauqua affairs. Henry Bailey's son, Jack, was a member of the Institution's Board of Trustees and since 1989, with his wife Diane, has been selling furniture, antiques, and accessories at Bailey's Interiors on the corner of Ames and Pratt. Henry Bailey's daughter-in-law, Helen M. Bailey, circa 1920, operated the original art and craft shop in the Colonnade Building. Currently his great granddaughter Gretchen Gaede owns and operates Gretchen's Gallery in the Colonnade.

The Quadrangle is a complex of studios in linear arrangement, each given to a separate discipline. A covered colonnade supported by cast concrete columns fronts the long, brown, shingle-sheathed structure, unifying the complex while enhancing its aesthetics. Together with lateral wings completed in 1916, it forms an open-ended courtyard. The many windows that open to the sheltered colonnade, together with those at the rear,

give the studios the feel of open-air workshops.

The quadrangle is a particularly lively place during classes, attended by artists with ages ranging from collegians to retirees. Here one senses the creativity that is part of the Chautauqua summer experience. Through a grant from Helen Temple Logan Trust, the Arts and Crafts Center was renovated in 1983 – roof, paint, brick pointing, and drainage system. In 2009 a complete renovation – new individual studios, expanded sculpture facilities, state of the art ceramic facility, printmaking shop, and fabulous drawing studio was funded by the Chautauqua Idea Capital Campaign. The Arts Center has over 50,000 square feet of studio and gallery space.

South Wing of the Arts and Crafts Quadrangle

Photo by Selden Campen

Arts and Crafts Quadrangle (continued)

The Arts and Crafts Quadrangle was built to house the Arts and Crafts School that the Institution started in 1902. The school now accepts each summer between 35 and 40 students with average age in the mid-twenties. In an interview in 2009, Arts and Crafts School Director, Don Kimes, said about the competitive selection process, "The decisive factor is not the prospective student's technical skills – it is motivation."

Chautauqua Arts Center West Wing Colonnade

Photo by Selden Campen

Joan Lincoln Ceramics Center adjacent to Quadrangle

Photo by Selden Campen

Kathleen Brien working on her "artist statement" at the Arts Quad

Photo from The Chautauquan Daily – Ruby Wallau Staff Photographer

Painters at Work on College Hill

Photo by Selden Campen

Students in Ceramics Studio

Photo by Selden Campen

Sheldon Hall of Education – 1884

Currently housing classrooms for Special Studies, the Sheldon Hall of Education was restored in 1998 through the generosity of the Sheldon Foundation. The two wings of this building, originally referred to as Annex A and Annex B, were built in 1884 on Pratt Avenue facing Harris Avenue, set near the proposed site of the College of Liberal Arts building, completed three years later. They were moved to their present location on

Photo by Selden Campen

Wythe Avenue adjacent to the Arts and Crafts Quadrangle in 1911. At this time a middle section was built to join the two, and the building was renamed The Hall of Pedagogy.

The Sheldon family's wealth was created in 1888 by providing, along with a small group of other investors, the initial capital and business expertise to form The American Aristotype Company in Jamestown, NY. The company developed and manufactured one of the first photographic papers produced in the United States. Extremely successful in the 1890's, American Aristotype attracted the attention of George Eastman as he was creating the Eastman Kodak Company. Eastman eventually bought the company and moved the manufacturing process to Rochester, New York in 1909. The decision to sell the company to Eastman Kodak was timely, as shortly thereafter their product became obsolete when superior printing papers were invented. After the company was sold, Ralph C. Sheldon became a banker, civic leader, and owner of Jamestown Newspaper Corporation, publisher of the local Jamestown newspaper.

Children's School – 1921/Fully Renovated in 1994

On Hurst Avenue between Wythe and Pratt Avenues is the Children's School, built in 1921 under the direction of architect Franklyn Kidd of the firm Green and Wicks, frequently employed by the Institution during that time frame. Additions have been made in 1926, 1947, 1969 and 1975. The covered pavilion in front of the school is reminiscent of the Hall of Philosophy, which also was designed by E. B. Green's firm.

Photo from The Chautauquan Daily – Greg Funka Staff Photographer

Children's School is a developmental preschool for youth ages three to six. The program has a wide range of social, recreational and educational activities. Weekly themes often incorporate music, drama, and art. The school has six classrooms (two at each age level) with a maximum of 30 students in each. Each classroom is staffed with two certified teachers and two college age and/or high school age assistants.

Nursery school education was pioneered at Chautauqua. According to

Photo by Selden Campen

Kit Trapasso, director of the Children's School, "Chautauqua found a wonderful niche, a program for young children and training for kindergarten teachers." By 1921, this program had evolved into a school with its own building. For children, Trapasso's priorities are comfort, community, creativity, and culture. A picture of the youngsters in the Children's School learning about our country's birthday and marching onto the stage on July 4th is included in the Amphitheater description earlier in the book.

Amber, Eli and Nathan supervised by father Weilun Cheng.

Photo by Selden Campen

Children's School behind "Hall of Philosophy"like pavilion.

Photo by Selden Campen

95

Lustron House – 1951

This fine, well maintained example at **23 Hurst Avenue** of a **Lustron House** has been owned by Zoe Barley since 2000. Walter and Margaret Bruce Horn built it in 1951.

Lustron homes are prefabricated enameled steel dwellings developed in the post-World War II era in response to the shortage of housing for returning GIs. The exterior color options were pink, tan, yellow, aqua, blue, green and gray. Interior options were beige or gray. A Lustron Corporation ad read, "You don't have to paint it, you can clean the walls with Windex, and you can hang things with magnets."

Photo by Selden Campen

Sponaugle/Gartner House – 2010

The home at **21 Hurst Avenue** started with a passion for collecting antique doorknobs that expanded into a growing expertise in architectural salvage. It culminated in the completion of the fascinating new home of Drs. Dale Sponaugle and Lou Ann Gartner.

The doctors bought their property across from the Children's School in 1992. The inspiration for his design of their house came when Dr, Sponaugle "was struck by the similarities between the curving pine boughs and a pagoda's elegant lines," he said.

Finding treasure in the architectural debris of others, Dale's unique avocation yielded a growing network of salvage suppliers and craftsmen. He began to stockpile wood, stone and artifacts for possible use in his dream house. In the end, 60 percent of materials used in construction were recycled.

Dr. Sponaugle pointed out, "Although materials and construction costs using recycled materials are higher, . . . we also got an insurance policy in some cases, for instance, we used more-than-100-year-old yellow pine to fabricate the beadboard-effect ceiling on the front porch. I know it's not going to warp or crack."

Stone for the new home came from six different demolished buildings in Buffalo. Wood includes maple, white oak, cedar, mahogany, Douglas fir, hemlock and yellow pine. Non-bearing walls defining the perimeter of the property are constructed of dry-stacked stone, pyramid-style, without mortar.

[Story adapted from a Chautauquan Daily article published on July 3, 2010]

Photo by Selden Campen

First Cottage – 1996

Ted and Deborah First's house at **43 Pratt Avenue** on the corner with Hurst was built in 1996. The preceding year, the Firsts constructed the exterior parts of this five-bedroom house in New Hampshire in sections and had them trucked here. Super insulated, the house is airtight and of unibody construction, so the First Cottage is hurricane, tornado, and earthquake resistant. Walls have nine-inch thick insulation, ceilings ten-inch thick insulation, and the basement contains polybutaline coils for heat, cedar shingles and wrap around spacious porches give this house its charm. Combined, collected, and homemade stained glass panels are incorporated into this well thought out home. Ted First has been active in Chautauqua County with Habitat for Humanity and has served on Chautauqua Institution's Architectural Review Board.

Photo by Selden Campen

Janson Cottage – 1904

Photo by Selden Campen

Located at **20 Hurst Avenue** on the northeast corner at Pratt, this cottage has much appeal due the unique oriental character of its roof, its commanding location and its attractive paint scheme. The treetop front porch posts remind one of the similar treatment of roof supports in the Amphitheater. The house was built by Sarah Kirk of Pittsburgh, Pennsylvania in 1904, and was purchased by Jennifer Jo Janson in 1984. The Janson House was built a century prior to the Sponaugle House diagonally across the street, which also sports an oriental roof.

Jewett House – 1886

Located at **20 McClintock** on the northeast corner of Pratt and McClintock Avenues, this Queen Anne style residence was built in 1986 by Mrs. A.H. Jewett for self-supporting young women, teachers and others who wanted to study at Chautauqua. For years it was used as a residence for students in the Summer Schools Programs, most recently by theater students.

The Queen Anne style is evidenced by its multi-gabled, intersecting roof elements, and in the touch of half-timbering in its top-most gable. The combination of clapboard and shingle affords variety in its wall surfaces.

Photo by Selden Campen

Vanderbeck Chapel – 1963

Photo by Selden Campen

The **Vanderbeck Chapel**, at **39 Pratt Avenue** near its intersection with McClintock Avenue was dedicated in 1963. The chapel is named after an outstanding International Order of the King's Daughters and Sons (IOKDS) leader, Ida A. Vanderbeck. The Chapel, an attractive accent to the Chautauqua scene with its small white spire, is in the Georgian Colonial Style. The Chapel is used for morning services and it is open to the public for quiet meditation. Below the Chapel is a reception hall, which also serves as a dining hall for the Summer Scholarship Student program. The IOKDS also maintains three dormitories: Benedict House at 34 Vincent, Florence Hall at 6 Irving Place and Bonnie Hall at 29 Vincent. In 1972, IOKDS moved its international headquarters to Chautauqua.

The IOKDS maintains an active summer scholarship program at Chautauqua and brings here each year outstanding students from many parts of the country and abroad. While they are here, the Chapel and its reception hall are at the center of their spiritual lives and other activities. The students typically assist the Chautauqua Religion Department as scripture readers during the weekday morning services and they also take part in Chautauqua's Special Studies Program. Many of these students have talents that they share by appearing on programs at Club or denominational house meetings throughout the summer.

Higgins Hall – 1905

Higgins Hall at **25 Wythe Avenue** was built and dedicated in 1905, the gift of State Senator F.W. Higgins of Olean, New York and his sister, Mrs. F.S. Smith of Angelica, New York, in memory of their father, Orrin Trail Higgins. It was designed as a lecture room with adjoining library, kitchen and parlor. The smaller rooms could be opened into the larger lecture hall to give greater seating capacity. At the dedication, Bishop Vincent said the hall was to be used for the programs of young girls at Chautauqua, but it has been used for many different activities, including art exhibits and recitals. Perhaps the most dramatic occasion was the formal breakfast that was given there in honor of President Theodore Roosevelt in 1905. His address in the Amphitheater that day was his first public statement after having been elected for his first full term as president.

Higgins Hall is used now for the Chautauqua Cinema, and it is air-conditioned. Ever since he was a youngster, Billy Schmidt had been behind the movie screen, up in the balcony, inside the film booth, and back in the little-known popcorn popping room at the Chautauqua Cinema. Schmidt is the third in his family to own and manage Chautauqua Cinema since 1956, following his father Paul and grandfather Robert.

Taking over the family business was not what Schmidt had in mind when he was attending Chautauqua High School, studying sound recording technology in college, and building the Cinema's screen stage with his father. For nearly 17 years, Schmidt went on tour with heavy metal bands in the U.S. and abroad. When the second of his two sons was born; however, he returned to his roots.

At Chautauqua, each Schmidt generation has kept current with technological change. On Bill Schmidt's watch, color digital cinematography has superseded film. By 2012, conversion to digital was imperative, as major studios were beginning to entirely eliminate 35mm film; yet the high cost seemed prohibitive. Schmidt followed his father's suggestion that he raise the $70,000 necessary for the conversion by offering lifetime tickets for $2,000 donations, lifetime popcorn for $500 donations and T-shirts for smaller donations. By the end of the 2012 season, Schmidt's fund-raising goal had been completed.

Schmidt said programming and promotion are

Photo by Selden Campen

now his biggest challenges. In choosing films for his Meet the Filmmaker Series, he works with the director of the Chautauqua Education Department and for the Classic Film Series, he works with David Zinman, Chautauquan and noted film historian.

Photo by Selden Campen

Wishful thinking - author and spouse featured in the movie

Photo taken and manipulated by Selden Campen

Photo by Selden Campen

School of Music Campus

Photo by Selden Campen

Chautauquans often speak about how the presence of young artists and musicians contributes to the atmosphere on the grounds. It seems as though creativity roams the avenues all day and far into the night, with music drifting out of this hall or that.

In 2007 the generosity of dedicated Chautauquans made possible an expansion and renovation of the School of Music. The renovations and new facilities have earned Chautauqua the endorsement of Steinway and Sons and the increased ability to recruit the highest-caliber students. Chautauqua is now one of four Steinway Festivals recognized nationally, and is judged as having the best facilities of any major music festival in the country.

The managing director of the School of Music can now schedule its thousands of events — including rehearsals, lessons and performances — far more efficiently, while at the same time increasing the school's ability to produce public programming. On most days there is a public event going on here at any time. Before 2005 there were perhaps three master classes a week.

In planning the renovations and construction, architects noted that a key aspect the School of Music lacked was a centralized campus. Having a music campus on the Institution grounds allows for more collaboration and easier communication within the department. Managing Director of the School of Music, Oliver Dow, said "It keeps the students much more contained — it's easier to communicate with them now, because they're mostly on the campus." Music School Festival Orchestra Conductor Timothy Muffet said, "We're bringing people together and there's a great synergy that's come through this."

Before Fletcher Music Hall was constructed and McKnight Recital Hall was renovated, music events were scheduled in halls that were not designed exclusively for musical purposes, including Smith Wilkes Hall and the Hall of Christ. Dow said, "I can schedule much more efficiently, because there are facilities which I directly have control over." Also, the combination of McKnight, Lenna and Fletcher halls near Palestine and Root Avenues has changed the Institution in a larger sense by increasing the flow of people to the north end of the grounds.

The practice shacks, longtime icons of music at the Institution, were also renovated. Each shack now boasts climate control. Oliver Dow said, "All of our students are intense about their work. Having a controlled environment makes a huge difference for the people practicing and for rehearsal." The School of Music staff agrees that the changes to the campus have had a huge impact on the quality of the program.

"Students who have returned to visit the facility after a number of years are astounded by the changes," said Marlena Malas, School of Music voice chair.

"Renovations to the Sherwood-Marsh Studios increased capacity in piano instruction from just two to five at a time," Rebecca Penneys, former School of Music piano chair, said. Penneys planted a memorial garden in honor of her parents around the Sherwood-Marsh Studios.

In total the 2008 major changes to the campus include four new facilities – Corry Hall, Cornell Hall, Office Depot Hall and Fletcher Music Hall – as well as the renovated Sherwood-Marsh Studios, Jane Pearson Hultquist Auditorium at McKnight Hall and the practice shacks.

[Adapted from a Chautauquan Daily article published on August 12, 2012]

Chautauqua file photo

School of Music Campus (continued)

McKnight Recital Hall – 1953/2008

McKnight Recital Hall, an arched roof structure built in 1953 and renovated in 2008, is used for recitals, master classes, and as a practice hall for the Music School Festival Orchestra and the Voice Department.

Chautauqua Archive file photo

Cory, Cornell & Office Depot Halls

Cornell Hall was named for Horatio Cornell, head of the Voice Department for 21 years. Built in 2008, these studios are used by the Summer Schools for vocal and instrumental practice space.

Photo by Selden Campen

Practice Village – Various Dates/2008

The 52 "**Practice Shacks**" were built over many years. By 1922 there were 39 buildings, 1 office, and 5 studios. They can't be called shacks anymore since they were air-conditioned, totally refurbished and endowed for $25,000 each in 2006. Number 38, located behind Lenna Hall, is where George Gershwin composed his "Concerto in F" in 1925.

Photo by Selden Campen

Statement by Nathan Gottschalk, Conductor – January 12, 1984 – Schenectady, NY

Chautauqua has played an important part in my music career and I am grateful that it continues to do so. In a sense, my presence at Chautauqua, since 1973, represents a second coming to that venerable Institution. I was a member of the Chautauqua Symphony Orchestra under Walter Stoessel and returned every summer until his passing. This also coincided with my entering the army. In 1973, I received an invitation to return to direct the Music School and develop the Festival Orchestra. I accepted the challenge enthusiastically. Since my return, I have received enthusiastic support from two administrations, which enabled me to build and develop an outstanding Festival Orchestra of college age talents. This has been, and continues to be, most fulfilling and enriching for me. I would also like to feel that the lives of the students and the entire Chautauqua community have been likewise enriched. Chautauqua is not only music, as everyone knows. Chautauqua has it all! – a kind of Gestalt experience. It is living a life of values. How can it not be a meaningful experience? Each year I look forward to doing my part to make it better than last summer. I know of no place quite like it.

Lenna Hall – 1993

Photo by Selden Campen

The Elizabeth S Lenna Hall, located at the corner of Hurst and Palestine Avenues, was a gift to the Institution from Reginald and Elizabeth Lenna of Jamestown, New York, then residents of Packard Manor. The facility is principally used for chamber music, voice and piano recitals, and for Chautauqua Symphony Orchestra and the Music School Festival Orchestra rehearsals. The building, completed in 1993, was the first major program venue constructed at Chautauqua in 64 years, since Norton Memorial Hall was built in 1929.

The 8,000 square foot hall can seat a recital audience of 500 people, and can be quickly converted to a larger stage area by raising the floor of the orchestra level seating to accommodate an orchestra of 100 musicians.

Great emphasis was given by the architect to create a hall with the best possible acoustics. Lenna Hall may be "tuned" with retractable acoustical curtains located in the high "hat shaped" roof.

Afternoon concerts at Lenna Hall are extremely popular. When planning to attend a chamber music event or special recital, it is prudent to arrive early to obtain seating on a first come, first served basis.

Painting by Robin K Robins — rkrobins@hotmail.com

Chautauqua Archive file photo

Photo by Selden Campen

Fletcher Music Hall – 2008

Fletcher Music Hall, Chautauqua's first "green" building, has solar panels on the roof providing electricity for both it and Lenna Hall. For these features of its design, the building won awards for conservation and protection of the environment. Fletcher Music Hall, completed in 2008 at Hurst and Palestine Avenues, is a gift of Robert and Ann Fletcher. The Fletchers responded to the Institution's need for additional performing and rehearsal space at the new Music School Campus.

Fletcher Music Hall provides indoor seating for 250 on retractable benches. When the seats are rolled back against the wall, the hall becomes essentially one large room. These two configurations provide great flexibility in its use. The building is winterized for use year-round. Initially built for the Summer School's Voice Department, Fletcher has many other users – two of which are the annual new play workshop staged by David Zinman, and the Robert H. Jackson Center of Jamestown, New York, seminars on current genocide cases which are or may be brought before International Tribunals.

Photo by Gena Bedrosian

Chautauqua archive photo – Roger J. Coda photographer

Rain Garden – 2008

Beginning with the "**rain garden**" at Fletcher Music Hall shown below, and that which replaced Hurst Avenue from Palestine at Hurst to the Brawdy Theater Studios near route 394, Chautauqua Institution has made efforts to improve the lake's water quality by slowing down and filtering rain run-off. The rain run-off otherwise would carry phosphates from fertilizer and other harmful chemicals with it as it flows down to the lake. Other significant gardens are from Palestine to Norton Hall, and at the base of Miller Park and College Hill.

Rain garden and path behind Fletcher Music Hall

Photo by Selden Campen

Path and adjacent gardens replacing upper Hurst

Photo by Selden Campen

Sherwood-Marsh Studios – 1912

Sherwood Music Studio was completed in 1912, designed by E.B. Green's architectural firm. The colonnade that partially surrounds it resembles the Arts and Crafts Quadrangle's front on Palestine. The studio was built as a memorial to William H. Sherwood, first head of the Piano Department at the Music School. It was reconditioned in 1966 by funds from Munger Aldridge, and substantially renovated in 2008 as a gift of the Marsh family. The Sherwood-Marsh Studios are beautifully renovated teaching and performing spaces within this historic structure.

In 2007, joining the ranks of Aspen, Brevard, and Tanglewood, Steinway and Sons designated Chautauqua its 4th and final Steinway Summer Festival. Each year Steinway makes available approximately 40 new pianos for use during Chautauqua's summer season.

The Sherwood Recital Room is a 100-seat space with a pair of well-matched Steinway Ds, and is used for group classes, master classes, weekly performance classes, and some competitions. In addition to the Recital Room, there are three teaching studios and two rehearsal rooms.

The premier and innovative Chautauqua Piano Program brings together a stellar kaleidoscope of guest faculty, and it has become a model for other summer piano festivals. Among them have been Rebecca Penneys, Alexander Gavrylyuk, Natalya Antonova, Jon Nokamatsu, Malcom Bilson and Evelyne Brancar.

Photo by Robert Cahn

Alexander Gavrylyuk conducting a master class in the The Sherwood Recital Studio.

Chautauqua file photo

103

Tennis Center – 2004

The Chautauqua **Tennis Center**, which opened in June 2004, is located directly behind the Turner Community Center on Route 394 and boasts eight state-of-the-art, fast-dry courts. Using the patented "Hydro-Grid" system, the clay-like playing surface is kept uniformly moist by a sub surface irrigation system. The result is a court that is consistent, gives a true bounce, is gentle on the feet and legs of players, and also drains exceptionally well, allowing for a quick return to play even after heavy rain. Two of the new courts are illuminated for night play. The new tennis center replaces the eight courts formerly located at the Main Gate. The American Sports Builders Association made the Chautauqua Tennis Center the recipient of their 2004 Outstanding Tennis Facility Award.

The pavilion was made possible by donations throughout 2008 to honor Dick Bechtolt's memory. Dick, an avid tennis player, was head of the "Dawn Patrol" – early morning players – and a former member of the Chautauqua Board of Trustees.

Photo by Selden Campen

Chautauqua file photo

Turner Community Center – 2000

Previously an elementary school and located at **4840 West Lake Road** west of the tennis courts, **Turner Community Center** now houses Special Studies classrooms, The Chautauqua Health and Fitness Center, basketball courts, and a 25-yard indoor swimming pool.

Acquired at the cost of $5 million to be paid at no interest over 18 years, it fulfilled a long-term dream of many dimensions. It substantially added classroom space, provided land away from the Main Gate for tennis, created new possibilities for a year-round conference center, and brought into better balance the facilities on the north versus south end of the grounds.

The Fitness Center has cardiovascular machines (treadmills, stair climbers, elliptical trainers, rowing machines, and bikes), strength training machines, free weights, and assorted other equipment. Staff, including certified trainers, are available to assist by appointment.

The swimming pool, kept at 82 degrees, has lockers, showers, and towel service, shared with the gymnasium – the latter available when not being used for classes or events.

The building is available year-round for community use. During the season, Turner serves as a gate to the grounds. Off-season, parking is available at Turner without charge.

Photo by Selden Campen

Photo by Selden Campen

Andriaccio's Restaurant – 1982

The Andriaccio family has its roots in the mountain village of San Fele, a rural area of Potenza Province in the Basilicata region. Vito Andriaccio immigrated in the 1870s from San Fele to the Myrtle Avenue neighborhood of Buffalo with his wife and nine children. Antoinette came to Buffalo at the age of two with her parents and sister from the village of Collepietro in the Abruzzi region of Italy.

Andriaccio's Restaurant at **4837 West Lake Road** has been serving the community and the many visitors that come to Chautauqua since 1982. The founders, Guy and Antoinette Andriaccio, along with their five children, moved to Chautauqua in the late '70s from Buffalo, where Guy had a restaurant on Chippewa Street. They bought an old gas station on Route 394 across from Chautauqua Institution and opened their doors in February of 1982. The restaurant has had many modifications and additions, the latest being the pergola added to the right side of the building in 2014.

Over the more than thirty years in business, the restaurant has seen founders Guy and Toni and their extensive family help out in one way or another, and the tradition continues today, as Nick and his wife Sally and their four children maintain the Andriaccio name, quality and pride, still providing the essentials that made them famous.

Walk into Andriaccio's and what's most apparent, besides the sweet aromas of homemade dough and fresh tomato sauce, is the wealth of family memorabilia hanging in the entry way: awards, newspaper clippings, family events, photos, reminders of the heart of Andriaccio's livelihood.

Photo by Selden Campen

Photo by Selden Campen

Photo by Selden Campen

Photo by Selden Campen

105

Tasty Acres of Chautauqua – 1944

Outside the Gate north of the Market Street entrance.

A popular diner at the Market Gate entrance to the Chautauqua Institution, **2724 West Lake Road**, had new owners in 2011, only the fourth such change since it began to do business 67 years earlier, in 1944. The eating place is now owned and operated by two veterans – Paul Smith and Nancy Embrcc.

The new owners rechristened the restaurant, previously known as Chautauqua Diner, to **Tasty Acres of Chautauqua**. Previous proprietors since it was first opened were the Grants for 13 years, the Wheelers for 27 years, and the Jacksons for 27 years. The new owners immediately installed a new furnace, added air-conditioning, installed carpet and painted. The result is evident in the immaculately maintained 1,600 square foot structure. It was a dining car, and if you take the sides off it is still there.

The dining room seats thirty-six at tables, while the counter seats an additional ten. They have a considerable regular clientele, several of which show up like clockwork and take their positions at the counter.

In the diner, there is a showcase that includes several newspaper stories about the restaurant's past. One such article is about Margaret Hamilton, who played a witch in the film, The Wizard of Oz, a faithful customer who helped Jim Jackson save his restaurant from the

Photo by Selden Campen

wrecking ball.

In 1979 the Institution wanted to tear down the diner for parking. At that time Margaret Hamilton was having three meals a day here. She went to the Institution's president, and talked to him about keeping the diner. "I don't know what she said, but we are still here," said Jackson.

Jackson served up favorites to a variety of rock stars and actors, who, like Hamilton, were visiting or performing at the Institution. This is still the experience of the current owners, but most interesting is the camaraderie among the customers.

Photo by Selden Campen

Photo by Selden Campen

Chautauqua Fire Hall and Police Department – 2006

Photo by Selden Campen

The Chautauqua Volunteer Fire Department and the Chautauqua Police Department share the same building with two different addresses.

The **Chautauqua Volunteer Fire Department** at **2 Royal Way** can be reached at 911 or (716) 357-3473. It protects the Town of Chautauqua as well as the Chautauqua Institution Grounds. This area has a winter population of approximately 2,500 and a summer population of up to about 12,000 per week. The district runs from Magnolia Road in the South to the Merz Boy Scout Camp in the North and from Chautauqua Lake on the East to County Road 25, Morris Road, on the West. It borders the fire districts of Mayville to the north, Ashville to the south and Sherman to the west that assist the Chautauqua Fire Department when and if the need arises.

In 2014 the Department responded to 430 calls, 200 of which were during the nine-week season at Chautauqua Institution. Its roster has 40 volunteers to service this volume of calls. New volunteers are always needed, but due to the time commitment required, are difficult to find. Volunteers put their lives in danger, but know they're helping to make Chautauqua a better safer community. "It's a sense of being, it's a sense of belonging, and it's a sense of being able to help your neighbor. There's not a greater feeling in the world knowing that you have the ability to help someone in need," said Fire Chief Adam Akin.

Chautauqua Police Department at **7 Massey,** open 9 a.m. to 5 p.m. during the season, can be reached at 911 or (716) 357-6225. For Chautauqua's veteran Police Chief Alan Akin, a visit to the Institution from then-President Bill Clinton in 1996 certainly stands out as a highlight of his career. "The size of the entourage, the excitement, the media buzzing all around," he recalled. "It was a lot of work, but it was fun." While the presidential visit stands out in his mind, Alan and his staff's routine work is what matters most to the Chautauqua community.

On the Chautauqua force since 1978, Chief Akin oversees four year-round, full-time police officers, three part-time officers and 10 seasonal bicycle patrolmen. Akin, who holds an appointment as a Chautauqua County deputy sheriff, has unprecedented depth and breadth of experience and expertise on his team. The officers have appointments as county special deputy sheriffs and have found their special niches on the force. Dan Hafner, for instance, is a member of the county forensic investigative team, in addition to handling Internet activity for the police. Noel Guttman is also a member of the county forensic investigative team, a grant writer, an emergency medical technician and assistant Mayville fire chief. Tammy Yager, an EMT with the fire department in Falconer, serves as the police station's office manager.

Akin seeks quality and continuity in his summer bicycle patrolmen. Like the arts and other programs at Chautauqua, the Police Department hires interns dur-

Firefighters respond to a 1994 Wensley House alarm

Photo by Selden Campen

Fire alarm call bell from and earlier day.

Photo by Robert Cahn

ing the summer both to man their force and to train as future law enforcement officers. "They are all college graduates or students who are headed for professional careers," he said. "We hope for, and usually get, six or seven each year who are returning,"

Officer Billy Leone said the type of incidents he sees today are the same he saw years ago: "Youths causing mischief, stolen bikes, a lot of parking complaints, a lot of alarms going off and crowd control." He said the Institution, while a safe place, has its fair share of theft and noise complaints, but the biggest challenge the police department faces is making sure crime doesn't happen.

[Police Department story adapted from
The Chautauquan Daily articles published
August 14, 2010 and July 14, 2012]

Bike Rent and Soap Opera Laundry

Photo by Selden Campen

Farmers' Market

The **Farmers' Market** is located on the north side of the building also shared by the Bus and Tram Office and the Lost and Found. Monday through Saturday local farmers and vendors bring their produce, baked goods and gladioli for sale to early risers. The **Lost and Found**, housed in the front left of the same building, makes an exhaustive effort to deliver to their rightful owners articles left behind. However, after a year, unclaimed low value items are sold, with proceeds going to the Chautauqua Fund. The **Bus and Tram Office** manages a fleet of buses and trams which, leaving from the Main Gate every 20 minutes, traverse the grounds in all directions offering free rides to patrons, helping to facilitate the on-premises vehicle restrictions enforced by the Institution.

This building was constructed in about 1900 as an electric plant, the Institution having outgrown the first electric powerhouse built along the lakefront in 1893. By 1903, the "new" plant needed an addition. Prior to its current use, the front of the building housed studios for instructors in string instruments, while the rear garaged Institution-owned work vehicles.

Photo by Selden Campen

The ever-popular **Bike Rent** shares a building with the **Soap Opera Laundry at 3 Massey Avenue**. Since 1987 Bike Rent has been owned and operated by Jamestown Cycle. Their charges are reasonable and in addition, bike rentals contribute an alternative transportation mode in support of the Institution's auto restrictive policies.

Bike Rent was initially owned and operated by Chautauqua teenagers. What a great way to acquire both mechanical and business skills while earning funds for college or other business pursuits. This began in 1976 when 14-year old Todd Lind founded Bike Rent and operated it out of his home at 14 Haven. In succession it was transferred to David Burgwardt (1977-1978), Melinda Burgwardt (1979-1982), and Stuart Johnston (1983-1986). The Burgwardts operated Bike Rent from their home at 17 Haven until 1982 when Melinda Burgwardt relocated Bike Rent to its current location on Massey.

On the side of the building is the Soap Opera Laundry, an Institution-owned laundromat operated for Chautauqua visitors, and a commercial laundry operated by and for the Athenaeum Hotel.

Photo by Robert Cahn

Photo by Robert Cahn

Chautauqua Governance

"The Committee" provided operational oversight of the Assembly prior to its being incorporated, i.e. 1874-1876. It was a special committee of the Methodist Episcopal Church Sunday School Union's Normal Department.

Members of The Committee are shown in front of the northern side of the original office building behind the auditorium, between the Speaker's platform and South Lake Drive, in the present-day Miller Park. We do not know whether the office building was deliberately taken down or if it was among the structures circling Miller Park consumed in the late 1880s fire.

Stereograph photo from the Chautauqua Archives

Now a 24-member board of trustees, four of whom are elected by property owners, governs the not-for-profit Chautauqua Institution. The board establishes the policies and direction of the Institution, electing the officers who are responsible for the operation of the Institution.

Daughter Chautauquas

Chautauqua has always considered accessible education to be essential to democracy. Through the summer programs and correspondence courses such as the Chautauqua Literary and Scientific Circle ("CLSC"), Chautauqua reached out to people across the continent and beyond.

With few accessible libraries and universities available, the CLSC offered many their first opportunity to obtain a college-level education by reading in their own leisure time. As the Chautauqua Idea grew in popularity, largely through the CLSC, people created Chautauqua programs in their local area. These came to be known as Daughter Chautauquas. By the early 20th century, there were at least 255 organizations that at one time or another associated themselves with the Chautauqua Movement. In addition, circuit Chautauquas traveled the country bringing programming to both rural and urban areas. These traveling Chautauquas offered a chance for a community to gather to enjoy a course of lectures. Audiences also saw classic operas and Broadway hits, and heard a variety of music from Metropolitan Opera stars to glee clubs to bell ringers. Most importantly, the circuit Chautauquas were critical in stimulating thought and discussion on important political, social and cultural issues of the day.

THE END
We Hope You Have Enjoyed Your Tour

Chautauqua Lake Sunday School Assembly Map
Chautauqua, New York – 1879

B I B L I O G R A P H Y

The Bestor Years (Not Dated)
> **Address of David McCullough: Chautauqua and Its Place in American Culture** (1993)
> by Alfreda L. Irwin, Chautauqua Institution – Chautauqua, New York

Chautauqua Archives (various property records, photos, etc.)
> archives.ciweb.org

The Chautauqua Assembly Herald and The Chautauquan Daily Archives (1876 to Present)
> www.chqdaily.com, Chautauqua, New York

Chautauqua Boys' and Girls' Club: Celebrating Our History as the Oldest Daycamp in the Nation (1999)
> by Rebecca Sample Habenicht and Gratia Habenicht Maley, Chautauqua Institution – Chautauqua, NY

Chautauqua Impressions, Architecture and Ambiance (1984)
> by Richard Newman Campen, West Summit Press – Chagrin Falls, Ohio

Chautauqua Institution – Postcard History Series (2011)
> by Jonathan David Schmitz and William Flanders, Arcadia Publishing – Charleston, South Carolina

Chautauqua Institution Website (various marketing brochures and other pamphlets and info on the Institution)
> www.ciweb.org

Chautauqua: Its Architecture and Its People (1978)
> by Pauline Francher, Banyan Books, Inc. – Miami, Florida

The Chautauqua Salute – A Memoir of The Bestor Years (1990)
> by Mary Frances Bestor Cram, Chautauqua Institution – Chautauqua, New York

The Chautauqua Story (1921)
> by Jesse L. Hurlbut, G, P. Putnam's Sons – New York, New York and Londen England

Chautauqua Vacation Homes (not dated)
> Women's Division, General Board of Global Ministeries of The United Methodist Church

Chautauqua Visitors Center Displays
> Post Office Building, Chautauqua, New York

The Everett Jewish Life Center in Chautauqua (2009)
> by Marisa Bulzone

The Endless Summers of Chautauqua (2002)
> by Marilyn Mathews Bendiksen
> The New York Archives Magazine – Summer 2002

Hidden Treasure: The Chautauqua Commisions of Buffalo's E.B.Green (2005)
> by Ed Evans, Falconer Printing and Design, Falconer, New York

Information on the Properties of the Order (1978)
> by Thelma A. Hauley, unpublished research paper, The Int'l Order of the King's Daughters and Sons

Official Walking Tour Guidebook of the Chautauqua Institution (1999)
> by Joan Fox and Dorothy Hill, Chautauqua Institution – Chautauqua, New York

Three Taps of the Gavel, The Chautauqua Story (1977)
> by Alfreda L. Irwin, Chautauqua Institution – Chautauqua, New York

Various Google Inquiries on Chautauqua Buildings, Persons, and Programs

Welcome to Chautauqua! A Walking Tour Guide of The Chautauqua Institution (not dated)
> by Anonymous, Chautauqua Institution – Chautauqua, New York

Index

Notes:

Notes:

WCTU – Before 1885

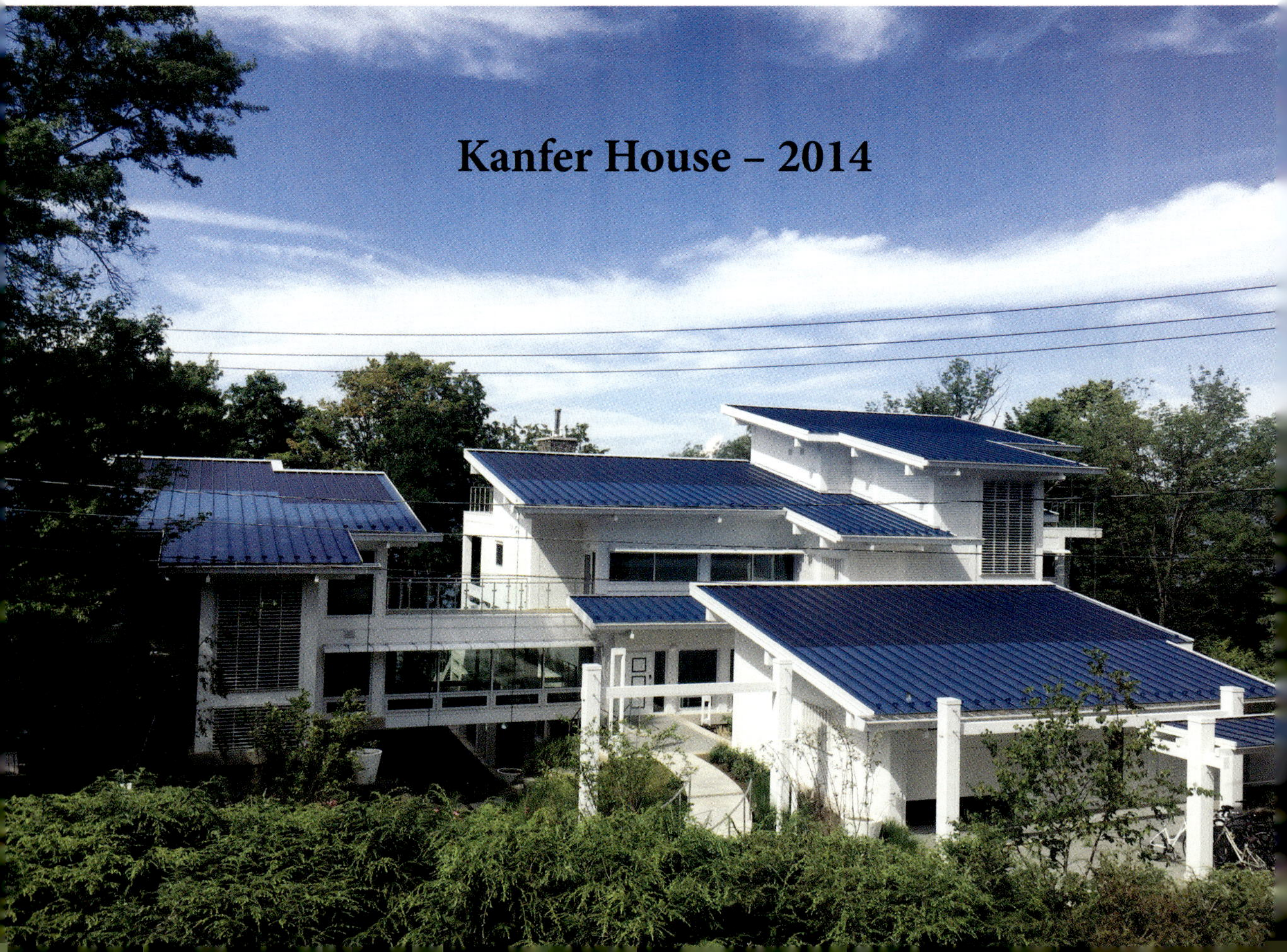

Robert Jeffrey

Kanfer House – 2014